No Hand To Hold &
No Legs To Dance On

Louise Medus and **Gill Swain**

Published by Accent Press Ltd – 2009

ISBN 9781906373573

Printed and bound in the UK

Cover Design by Red Dot Design

Cover photograph by Darryl Corner

Other photographs: author's collection

For Emma, Jack, Darren and my mum and dad.

Preface

THE ASTONISHING STORY OF thalidomide must surely be the worst medical disaster in history: a pill which caused devastating birth defects even if a pregnant woman took it only once. A pill which was aggressively marketed as "completely safe" and particularly suited to treat nausea or sleeplessness in expectant mothers without any research being done to support those claims. Looking back from a modern perspective when health and safety standards are so rigorous, partly as a result of the thalidomide disaster, it seems almost unbelievable, the stuff of science fiction.

It was hard, cruel fact, however, and its savage effects had to be borne by thousands of children and their families across the world. Thalidomide was a phenomenally successful drug – by the time it was banned 64 million tablets had been sold – and it resulted in an epidemic of babies born with shortened, flipper-like limbs in place of their arms and legs. What is less well known because it is less visible is that the limb damage was only part of the story. Some babies suffered brain damage or impairment to their eyes, ears and internal organs or facial paralysis, conditions which could be even harder to deal with than limb reduction. In all cases the babies' entry into the world, born to parents eagerly looking forward to meeting their beautiful new baby, was greeted by a range of the deepest emotions: profound shock, heart-rending pity or, sometimes, appalled horror.

Some parents screamed when they first set eyes on their thalidomide child. Fathers fainted dead away. Nurses were

1

sometimes so overwhelmed by the enormity of the task of breaking the news that they kept the babies wrapped and the parents only discovered the truth when they got home. There were stories of parents finding it impossible to cope and abandoning their babies; of fathers declaring that if their wives brought that "monster" home, they were leaving – and of some carrying out the threat; of couples doing their parental duty but only with great difficulty. Yet for all those who reacted with horror, there were far more parents who were flooded with a tide of love and protectiveness towards their helpless offspring and who brought them up to make the most of life. As for the babies, some were so deformed internally they died soon after birth but those who survived for the most part tackled life with gusto.

Many of the most severely afflicted, lacking all four limbs, were told they were not likely to survive childhood, then that they would die before they were 21, or 30, or 40. Now the "Thalidomiders", as they call themselves, are all approaching their 50s and leading full lives; they have worked, brought up children. In short they have lives packed with the same rich range of joys and sorrows as anyone else.

Their amazing and humbling achievements have been accomplished against a backdrop of the massive changes in attitudes towards the disabled in society which has taken place since the early 60s. Disabled people used to be pitied, feared and shut away from sight in big institutions, but all that has undergone a revolution. With the help of modern technology they have come out from behind closed doors and now mostly live independent lives, contributing their own unique talents and energies to the benefit of society. They accept themselves as they are and make the most of what they have and in general society has come round to accepting them.

So how did a drug with such appalling consequences for the developing foetus ever come to be put on the open market? Until now the accepted wisdom has been that the manufacturers could not have predicted that it would cause birth defects but new research, currently being undertaken by the Thalidomide Trust, may result in allegations of criminal negligence.

In the post-war era of the 1950s, science and invention seemed to be delivering a brave new world of nothing but good things. It was a time when almost every home began to acquire a washing machine, a refrigerator and a television, when computers were being developed and space travel began. In the world of medicine, the increasing use of penicillin in the 1940s was followed by a race to find new antibiotics, hailed as the miracle cure for the deadliest diseases known to man.

It was also when the first mood-altering drugs to receive the stamp of medical legitimacy were produced. Tranquilizers and sleeping pills – the "mother's little helpers" of the time – became widespread. In Britain around a million people used some kind of sedative daily in the mid-50s and around one in eight of National Health Service prescriptions were for sleeping pills. The problem was that most tranquilizers were dangerous barbiturates and deaths from deliberate and accidental overdoses were rising alarmingly.

A company called Chemie Grunenthal, a sister company of a large, family-owned cosmetics company in Stolberg, near Aachen, West Germany, was trying to develop new drugs to take advantage of the rapidly expanding sedative market. According to the account in *Dark Remedy*, by Rock Brynner and Trent Stephens, the company's director of research and development, Dr Heinrich Muckter, a former medical scientist in the German army, worked with the chief of chemical research, Wilhelm Kunz, mixing organic compounds to find something with pharmacological potential. Kunz, a former army sergeant, had been given his position despite having little scientific background.

Some time in early 1954, so the account goes, Kunz heated a chemical called phthaloylisoglutamine which changed its molecular structure. He and Muckter gave the drug that resulted the name thalidomide then looked around for a condition that it could cure. This may seem a curious way of doing things to the layman but was pretty standard procedure amongst drug manufacturers at the time.

Initial trials were disappointing as the drug had little effect on animals, not even acting as a sedative. But the researchers were excited by the observation that it appeared to be completely non-toxic: even at extremely high doses, it did not kill rats. Muckter therefore authorised the company's pharmacologist, Dr Herbert Keller, to try it as a sedative for humans. Instead of conducting proper, controlled trials, however, the company simply distributed free samples through doctors and handed out pills to their employees, without any monitoring or follow up. One observer commented: "Thalidomide was introduced by the method of Russian roulette. Practically nothing was known about the drug at the time of its marketing."

The result was that the first thalidomide baby, a little girl with no ears, was born on Christmas Day, 1956, the daughter of an employee of the company who had taken home some of these samples when his wife complained of morning sickness early in her pregnancy. No one had an inkling of the connection at the time and the human trials were showing that thalidomide induced a hypnotic, deeply relaxed sleep. Many physicians were impressed and Grunenthal was so excited by its potential that on October 1, 1957 they launched it, under the patent name Contergan, without prescription, with an enormous publicity campaign including 250,000 personal letters to doctors calling it a "wonder" remedy, perfectly safe and with no side effects. Success was immediate and widespread: by 1961, thalidomide was the best-selling sedative in Germany, sales represented half the company's income and their staff numbers had tripled.

In July, 1957 the giant Distillers company, best known for manufacturing alcoholic drinks, acquired the rights to market the drug in the UK and throughout the British Commonwealth. So eager was the company to get the drug on the market it accepted a licence deal which allowed no time to do its own trials and it began distributing thalidomide under its own trade name, Distaval, in April, 1958. The drug was advertised as "completely safe," the ideal solution to the "mounting toll of barbiturate deaths". Eventually thalidomide was sold in 46 countries under at least 37 names. In August,

1958 Grunenthal wrote to German physicians declaring that thalidomide was the best drug for pregnant and nursing mothers, a claim copied on the Distaval label by Distillers without any scientific foundation.

Grunenthal and the other companies around the world persisted in aggressively pursuing this line of marketing despite the fact that there *were,* in reality, complaints from patients of side effects from early on. By the end of 1958 some physicians in Germany were reporting to Grunenthal that certain patients taking Contergan suffered dizziness, cold hands, feet turning numb, memory loss, trembling, constipation and decreased blood pressure. In October, 1959 a Dusseldorf neurologist called Dr Ralf Voss wrote asking the company if anyone had reported that their wonder drug caused polyneuritis – a numbness and tingling in the hands and feet which was affecting one of his patients. Heinrich Muckter and Gunther Sievers from the company replied that they had received no complaints of that nature, which was a deliberate lie. In fact, by the end of 1960 the company had received around 100 reports of nerve damage attributable to thalidomide.

Voss continued to suspect Contergan and in April, 1960 he reported to a conference of neurologists in Dusseldorf about three patients who had developed the nerve damage condition, polyneuritis – also called peripheral neuritis or neuropathy – after using the drug. Monitoring his patients over the following year, he never saw any of them recover their lost feeling – the damage done by thalidomide seemed to be permanent. Soon his voice was joined by others, including some British doctors. Pressure grew on Grunenthal at least to put thalidomide under prescription and some German hospitals banned it. But the company never ordered further research in response to these reports; instead it did its best to discredit them, cover them up and create confusion so it could continue to rake in huge profits.

Meanwhile, babies with severe and shocking birth defects were being born across Germany. The first one to be recorded as a case history was in December, 1959 when a Dr Weidenbach described a girl whose arms and legs were so shortened that her hands and feet were attached directly to her body. The condition is called "tetra phocomelia", literally "four seal's limbs", and occurs naturally in an estimated one in four million births. Other doctors who were seeing similar babies each thought it was a one-off, a sad but very rare genetic malfunction. At the same time in Britain, Distillers were sending out promotional leaflets about Distaval to physicians with no mention of the problems with polyneuritis and announcing boldly: "Distaval can be given with complete safety to pregnant women and nursing mothers without adverse effect on mother or child."

On the other side of the world, however, the link was being made. Three women patients of Dr William McBride, who ran one of the largest obstetrics practices in Australia, gave birth within a month to babies with remarkably similar defects including missing bones in the forehead and blocked bowels, all of whom died. After the third death Dr McBride made a thorough study of his patients' hospital records and discovered the one common denominator was that the mothers had taken Distaval in pregnancy. He was convinced that was the cause. As soon as he could, he phoned Distillers and told a representative of his conclusions. He always subsequently insisted that he also sent a paper to the British medical journal *The Lancet*, but the journal unfortunately has no record of receiving it. This was in June, 1961 around four months before a beautiful young pregnant woman in London called Vicki Mason was to take Distaval to help her sleep. Had that paper been published, much suffering would have been prevented and her daughter, Louise, would have had a very different life.

By the end of 1961 the connection was made in Germany, too. A young lawyer called Karl Schulte-Hillen had both a daughter and niece born with phocomelia and had sought an explanation from Professor Widukind Lenz, head of the children's clinic at Hamburg University, who had already been sent details of a similar case. Astonished at this cluster of what were usually extremely rare defects, the pair put adverts in newspapers appealing for information about other cases and

Lenz began painstakingly trawling through the city's birth records and contacting the mothers of similarly disabled children. In subsequent interviews, one of the mothers mentioned taking Contergan during pregnancy; by November he had come across 14 cases where thalidomide was a common factor. He called Dr Muckter at Grunenthal and told him that Contergan should be withdrawn immediately. He said that every day the drug remained on the market was a deliberate experiment in human teratology.

In Australia, also in November, 1961, Dr McBride wrote again to the Lancet and this time his paper was published. In Germany, Professor Lenz told other physicians he believed Contergan was responsible for the epidemic of birth defects and met Grunenthal representatives at the Ministry of Interior where officials ordered the company to withdraw the drug from sale or they would ban it. Grunenthal refused, resisted all pressure and sent out another 70,000 leaflets to doctors insisting "Contergan is safe" until a major newspaper, *Welt am Sonntag*, broke the news of Lenz's findings on November 26, 1961. They cited his letter to Grunenthal which said: "Every month's delay in clarification means that fifty to one hundred horribly mutilated children will be born."

Grunenthal then had no alternative but to withdraw thalidomide from the German market and within a week Distillers followed suit. No one knows exactly how many thalidomide babies were born but current estimates put the figure at 15-20,000 of which perhaps a third did not survive beyond their early teens. There were nearly 3,000 known victims in Germany and over 650 in the UK. Even today some are still coming forward.

So, with the damage finally having been halted, the time came for the accounting. In May, 1968 nine Grunenthal executives were put on trial – one of the prosecutors was Karl Schulte-Hillen. The case dragged agonisingly on for two and a half years until the company claimed it could go bankrupt, leaving no money to compensate the victims, so proceedings were suspended "in the public interest". Towards the end of 1970, the West German parents accepted an offer of

$31million which was topped up with a further $13million by their government.

In Britain it took much longer, partly because after the first law suit was filed by 62 families against Distillers on November 7, 1962, the press was subject to a "gagging order" forbidding any mention of thalidomide while the case was being considered. After seven years of wrangling, the company offered an indecently small out-of-court settlement of an average £15,000 per child only to the 62 families in the original suit. To the rest they said they would pay £1,500 to each set of parents and set up a charitable trust of £3,750,000, the interest from which would be distributed amongst them annually. But there were two astonishingly draconian conditions – the offer must be kept confidential and it must be accepted by every single family: if only one refused to sign, no one would get a penny.

This condition acted like a red rag to a bull to wealthy London art dealer David Mason, whose daughter, Louise, was born with severely restricted arms and legs in 1962. At a mass meeting in London he and four other families courageously withstood the considerable pressure from the company, the lawyers for both sides and all the other parents present by refusing to sign to accept the offer. Furious at what he saw as immoral blackmail, Mason determined to take the fight to the press. *The Sunday Times* was already investigating the story but the first newspaper actually to take the bold step of defying the gagging order was the *Daily Mail* whose then editor, David English, was a friend of a friend of Mason's. Though English risked going to prison, the paper published a story: "My Fight for Justice – by the Father of Heartbreak Girl Louise" on December 20, 1971. English was not arrested but it was almost a year later, in September, 1972, when *The Sunday Times*, under its campaigning editor Harry Evans, also mustered the courage to challenge the law by launching one of the most powerful and effective campaigns in British publishing history with a story entitled "Our Thalidomide Children: a National Shame".

David Mason became the public face of the campaign for a settlement which would properly compensate the thalidomide victims for loss of earnings during their lifetime and guarantee them a comfortable standard of living. Tall, good-looking and forceful, he was a charismatic campaigner who took every opportunity to appear on TV or radio and to give interviews to the press. Meanwhile Jack Ashley, a deaf Labour MP, began an impassioned campaign in the House of Commons and a group of ten concerned Distillers' shareholders recruited others, including some large companies, to demand the company act responsibly.

Under this relentless pressure, Distillers gradually increased their offer until in April, 1973 they finally came up with an acceptable package amounting to £26 million, including an element for inflation, and the Government then added an extra £5 million to offset any future tax liabilities – a total of almost ten times the amount that Distillers originally offered in settlement. A measure of how necessary this enormous campaign was is that victims of thalidomide in Spain and Italy have never received a penny in compensation because there has never been a public campaign to demand it.

The creation of thalidomide and the struggle to gain justice for its victims had a profound impact on the public's attitude to medicine – until then scientists and doctors had been trusted to know best and do things right. This was the first example of serious physical harm being done by a supposed medical advance. Afterwards the notion that a doctor is necessarily always right had gone for ever and the belief that scientific advances in medicine were exclusively for the good was shattered. Far more rigorous testing on animals, particularly primates, was introduced for new medicines, which has resulted in its own controversy over the ethics of using animals in research.

While this was going on the surviving thalidomide children grew up and tackled the problem of how to make a life for themselves, and on the whole it has been a remarkable success story. Most of them have done useful work, forged relationships and had families of their own. Fifty years after thalidomide went on the market they are now entering middle age and have launched a new fight to get additional funds to pay for the appliances and adaptations they will need as age takes its toll.

This year David Mason's daughter, Louise Medus-Mansell, will be 47. Married last year for the second time, she has two children by her first marriage, does volunteer work she loves and plays a valuable part in her community, but it has not been an easy ride. Her story typifies the struggles many Thalidomiders have been through and the triumphs they have achieved.

While the compensation battle was raging in the 1970s, the MP Jack Ashley asked in a parliamentary debate how Louise, then 11 years old, could ever look forward to "laughing and loving with no hand to hold and no legs to dance on".

Well, says Louise, "I have danced. I have held hands with a lover. I have married and had my two wonderful children. I have worked, I have played, I have loved and been loved and I've been hurt. It's a full life, just like anyone else's but more precious to me in its ordinariness, perhaps, because that very normality has been a struggle to achieve."

This is her story.

Chapter One
The Shock Of My Birth

MY PARENTS WERE EXPECTING many things of their first-born child. It was before the days of scans so they didn't know if they were having a boy or a girl but they expected any offspring of theirs to be tall, handsome and healthy, as they both were, and probably clever and charming too. What they certainly did not expect was me.

I cannot possibly imagine what my dad, David Mason, thought or felt when a grim-faced doctor led him to a delivery room in the maternity hospital half an hour after my birth on June 23, 1962, showed him his tiny baby daughter lying swaddled in a cot and then slowly unwrapped the blanket. All I know is that he almost fainted from shock when I was fully revealed and blurted out, "Surely you're not going to allow a child in this state to live!"

You can hardly blame him. He was aware there had been a spate of children being born with dreadful deformities over the previous few years but he never expected – who does, after all? – such a terrible thing to happen to him and my mum, Vicki, who was then lying heavily sedated in the delivery room having been told only that her child had been born "not fully formed".

Both very young – my dad was 22 and my mum just 21 – they had a Posh and Becks kind of glamour at a time when the Sixties were just beginning to swing and they were very much in love having been married only a year. My mum was dark-haired, slim, extremely pretty and fashionable in the Mary

Quant style of miniskirts, big false eyelashes and pale lipstick. She had been offered work as a model but had decided to become a secretary instead.

She came from a well-to-do working-class family, originally from Wigan, Lancashire. My grandpa, Jack Whiteside, was a fruit and vegetable distributor who had moved his family down to London when she was a child to be nearer to Covent Garden, which was the centre of his trade. She was the elder of two daughters, they were strict Catholics and she had a sheltered, comfortable and loving upbringing and was innocent, joyful, enthusiastic and humorous.

My dad was 6ft tall, blond, handsome, ambitious and dynamic. He worked with his father, a successful London art dealer, and was determined to expand the business. His maths was chronic – he once told me that when he did an exam he was actually marked 0% – but he knew where he wanted to go and above all he knew art because he had learned the trade thoroughly from his father.

My parents met through my dad's sister, Di, who worked as an air hostess with my mother's sister, my Auntie Hilary. This was before the days of the Pill and free love so to be together they had to get married. It was not long after the wedding when my mum discovered she was pregnant and gave up work to be a full-time mother. My dad had to give up something too – he was a very enthusiastic and pretty successful amateur racing driver but, after some persuasion, he realised that his impending responsibilities meant he couldn't be so reckless with his life any more.

So they were a joyful, fortunate couple, revelling in the new experience of running their first home, a smart two up, two down in Cuffley, Essex, and with the world in front of them. They've both got a great sense of humour and banter and tease each other all the time, even all these years later. Expecting their first baby was very exciting and they spent many happy hours imagining what their child would look like and who he or she might take after.

They had got my bedroom decorated and Dad painted the cot, which Mum found very amusing as DIY was not his strong point and he got so much paint on it that it had to be taken to a professional to strip it down and start again. Mum bought both blue and pink clothes, blankets, toys and so on and dutifully attended all the ante-natal clinics.

I know about all this partly from reading my dad's book: *Thalidomide, My Fight*, which came out when I was 13, and partly from one conversation I had with my grandpa's sister, my Auntie Avis. I learned very early on not to broach the whole subject of my birth and the way I am with my parents because it is still so difficult for them to talk about. If I ever do bring it up, I immediately see in their eyes the deep hurt that the memory of my arrival dredges up.

I liked listening to or reading about these stories of how happy and excited they had been by the pregnancy because it made me feel that I was wanted, at least before I was born. But I also asked Auntie Avis how my mum reacted to my actual arrival and she said she went from being "a happy-go-lucky girl to somebody who was depressed and shocked and built a wall around herself". That wall between her and me is still there; I have peeped through it once or twice but, whenever I do, she hastily builds it up again. I can see her quite clearly constructing it, brick by brick.

My mum sailed through the pregnancy except for a short period early on when she was not sleeping well and was waking in the morning feeling exhausted. Her GP prescribed Distaval, hailed as a wonder drug for its properties as a mild sedative which helped to cure sleeping problems without unwelcome side effects.

Nothing else was wrong until her second to last ante-natal examination when a student doctor examined her by feeling her bump, as was the only method in those days. Mum was quite happy for him to do this as she was a great believer in medicine and liked to help young doctors to learn by experience but she grew alarmed when he began to look worried and confused.

Unsurprisingly, she felt a whole lot worse when the student called a consultant and said he couldn't feel the baby's arms and legs. The consultant re-examined her, said everything was fine then put down the upstart student in the typical way, pointing out witheringly that here were the arms and there the legs.

My mum was pretty upset after the appointment though my dad did his best to reassure her that the consultant must know best. Still worried, she talked to Grandpa who was friends with a gynaecologist, Dr Keith Evans, who worked in a hospital in Rochdale, Lancashire.

Grandpa gave him a ring and Dr Evans also assured the family that the consultant would definitely know better than the student so nothing more was said. Mum could feel me kicking and, if you've never had a pregnancy before, a kick is a kick whether it's from a proper leg or not. But, still, I think my mum knew that there was something not quite right. You do, don't you?

Mum started going into labour two weeks early and Dad drove her to Chasefield Farm Hospital in Enfield, Middlesex, where she was booked in to give birth. In those days fathers were kept out of the delivery room so he went off to buy a huge bouquet of flowers in a basket plus two ribbons, one coloured pink and one blue, one of which he planned to tie on the handle once he knew the sex of the baby.

The labour was long and my dad had spent many anxious hours pacing the corridor outside the delivery room when in the early hours of the morning a grave young doctor emerged and, without looking him in the face, gently put his arm around my dad and led him into his office.

There he told him that his child was alive. My dad, realising something must be dreadfully wrong for the doctor to have stated this one fact so baldly, frantically asked him what on earth he meant. The doctor hesitantly told him that I wasn't completely developed and that I "wasn't quite ready to be born." He added that "the arms and legs are not complete" and that I also had a birthmark across my face and jaundice.

Completely devastated, my dad started gabbling questions: "How did this happen? Is my wife OK? Is the baby OK? Can I see the baby? Is it a girl or boy? Is it going to live?" The doctor explained that he didn't know my mum's medical history and that my dad would have to speak to her G.P. in the morning to find out if something had caused this disaster.

He went on to add, "Yes, you can have a quick look. Yes, your wife medically is going to be OK. The baby is a girl." Then he broke the news no parent ever wants to hear: "No, she isn't OK." He said it would be unlikely that I would live for more than a day or two and if I did I would probably be a "cabbage" and need total care for the rest of my days.

While the doctor was talking to my father, my mother was begging for her baby to be brought to her and was being gently but adamantly refused and heavily sedated. I didn't fully understand the absolute hell that that must have been for her until I had my own daughter, Emma, and she was taken from me one night and put in the hospital nursery. I felt my heart had been ripped right out of me and I would never allow it to happen again.

Mum had been moved to a ward when my dad was taken into the delivery room and introduced to me. At first he thought I looked quite normal but then the stark truth was unveiled and he saw what he described in his book as "a tiny torso with what appeared to be four flowers sprouting from the corners."

I am a phocomelic, which is a word from Greek literally meaning "seal limbs" and refers to the fact my arms and legs are like flippers. I have got no long bones in either my arms or my legs because the thalidomide stopped them growing at a couple of inches. My hands and feet then developed on the ends of the stumps.

My legs are about two and a half inches long – the left is actually a quarter of an inch longer than the right – with feet which are turned up and twisted into my body so that my feet are actually on top of my legs. I've got five toes on each foot but placed the wrong way round, that is the big toe is where the little toe should be, which makes wearing socks rather uncomfortable.

I've got no bone in my left arm, just muscle, but I can flip it up and down and I use it to steer my wheelchair. I've got some bone in my right arm so I can reach out for things and grasp them quite firmly. I've got three fingers on my left hand and four on my right – in the wrong order, like my toes – and no thumbs. Most Thalidomiders have got no thumbs. I'm two foot six inches fully stretched out and big boned.

The other disfigurements which my dad took in with that first glance were a bright pink birth mark stretching all the way down my face and across from my right ear to my left ear, which you can still see, especially when I am either very hot or cold. I also have a flattened nose which is a characteristic of a lot of Thalidomiders and many of us have had to have operations to ease our breathing. And my skin was sort of yellowish from the jaundice.

I say I can't imagine how he felt as he looked at me, his daughter, because in the first place, I am not a man and I have come to realize that men's minds work completely differently to women's. I think it hit his male pride, his ego; that he felt it was his fault that I was an imperfection. Everything else in his life was perfect: he had a perfect wife, a perfect marriage, a perfect job, and there was I, not perfect by a long way.

This would have been going on subconsciously, of course. I think I can picture his conscious thoughts while he was plummeting from cloud nine to shell-shock which must have been along the lines of: "O God! What is she going to do? How will she live? Will her arms and legs carry on growing now she's born?"

He and the doctor thought there had never been anything like me in history but, actually, there had (apart from the other Thalidomiders). In Victorian times there was a chap known as the Caterpillar Man who was displayed in travelling shows as a freak. He was a coloured man, born without arms or legs, whom they dressed in a green knitted suit and made him wriggle on the floor like a caterpillar. It is now thought that he suffered from a genetic disorder which produced deformities similar to thalidomide.

When my father made his "you're not going to allow her to live" remark, three nurses quickly stepped between him and me and the doctor led him outside where he calmed down and began to feel terrible for what he had said.

I think it was natural, however, and I know that in times past it was commonplace for midwives or other people quietly to dispose of babies as disabled as I was, usually by smothering. Also, when I was a young teenager, which was the time when I really started thinking about how I was and what had happened to me, I was very keen on animals and kept a whole menagerie.

I compared what my parents did with how animals behaved and worked it all out in terms of instinct. For instance, I bred a lot of hamsters and I'd seen that if one was born with a bad paw or some other imperfection which would make survival difficult, the mother would leave it out to die or even deliberately kill it.

Understanding the reasons for the way they reacted in the context of animal instinct has helped me cope with the hurt. I have a little cupboard inside me in which I hide all my painful emotions. So something hurts, I cry, I store and I close the door and that's it. The memories never go away, however. Occasionally the door opens slightly and the pain slips out but I've learned to shut it again quickly and firmly because I've been hurt so many times.

Anyway, back to my dad who was in a state of profound shock, grief and turmoil as he roared away from the hospital and headed for the house of the GP who had diagnosed the pregnancy, stopping only to sling the big basket of flowers and the blue and pink ribbons over a garden fence.

It was 4 a.m. but he hammered insistently on the door until the bleary-eyed GP appeared in his dressing gown and slippers wondering what on earth was going on. Seeing Dad looking wild and ashen-faced, he let him in and listened to the whole story. Dad demanded to know what could possibly have caused such a disaster so the GP got out Mum's medical records and one glance told him what had happened. "Oh my God, I gave your wife Distaval," he groaned.

He pulled out a copy of the medical journal *The Lancet* and showed Dad an article about Distaval, which was one of the proprietary names for thalidomide, and how it had been connected with lots of deformed babies. Also, on May 26,

1962, just under a month before I was born, the government had realized the connection between thalidomide and the epidemic of damaged babies being born across Europe and had issued a public warning against Distaval, urging people to throw away immediately any remaining unused tablets. My dad went berserk, though I suspect a tiny part of him was relieved that it wasn't any kind of impurity in him which had caused my problems.

The next morning he faced the nightmare ordeal of having to tell Mum that the sleeping pill she had taken had damaged their baby. She became completely hysterical and demanded over and over again to see me but the doctors were still convinced I would not live.

In those days it was thought a mother would recover emotionally and psychologically more quickly from a stillbirth or neonatal death (a baby dying in the first two weeks of life) if she didn't see or cuddle the child. It's absolute rubbish and I don't know how they could ever have thought such a thing, but so it was and so they continued to refuse to bring me to her.

Over the next ten days a nurse would pop in occasionally with another strong sedative and Mum would ask plaintively, "How's my baby?" but she was told nothing except that I was as well as could be expected.

She could get no more out of my dad who was also trying to protect her. Both of them believed in medical authority which was telling them with one voice that this was the best thing and Grandpa backed the doctors too. She was too distressed and sedated to fight them all.

It must have been an absolute torment for her. I suspect she lay there for hours thinking, not fully formed – what does that mean? Does she have no head, no bottom, no eyes, no ears? Is she still in a foetal state, does she look like a monster? What have I produced?

Things have swung completely the other way now and there would be uproar if the same thing happened today. The papers would be full of headlines screaming about a "mum deprived of her baby" and there would be law suits and all sorts of fuss. I feel angry that doctors and society in general then didn't realize how vital it is for emotional health to establish the bond between a mother and child in the first few days after birth. And that disabled children are exactly the same in this regard as anyone else.

As I was expected to die, Mum sadly agreed that I should be baptized with the name she and Dad had chosen for a girl, Louise, and the ceremony was performed quietly in a hospital room. Meanwhile Dad and Grandpa had been talking to Grandpa's gynaecologist friend, Dr Keith Evans, who offered to take me into his care at Birchill Hospital in Rochdale, and also advised them to get my mum home and to carry on refusing to let her see me at all costs. So Dad, Grandpa, and a nurse wrapped me up and drove me the 220 miles to Rochdale.

By the time I was two weeks old my jaundice had gone and I was doing very well, eating, crying and making all the healthy signs a baby should make. It became clear that I would live, and this has become a bit of a pattern for us Thalidomiders through the years.

People predicted that we wouldn't live more than a few days, then it was a few months, then a year, then two, then that we wouldn't see our teens, then our twenties, then thirties. By the time we hit our forties, the doom-mongers gave up because we are still here. If a few of us start dying in our late sixties you can expect to see the fortune tellers coming out again with the prediction "No Thalidomiders live beyond 70." We won't take much notice whatever they say because we've got used to the fact that every day that we live we are making history.

Once it was established that I was sticking around for a little while at least, my parents faced the dilemma of what to do with me and again looked to the professionals for informed advice. Dr Evans gave his opinion that it would be madness for them to try to look after me because even if they could cope when I was a baby there would surely come a time as I grew bigger that they couldn't and then it would be cruel to send me away after I was used to life at home. According to my dad's account, his opinion was backed by the paediatrician and the psychiatrist at Birchill too.

My mother was in agonies, thinking one minute she could look after me and the next minute that she couldn't, right up until the last moment. They would have had enough money to hire help but the question is: would they have been mentally strong enough to cope and would their marriage have survived? Many parents of Thalidomiders divorced because of the strain.

I think my mum may have been able to find the strength but she was dominated by my far more forceful dad and grandpa and she had not established the connection with me which might have given her the ammunition to fight them. I am not sure my dad would have coped. His pride had been hurt and he was a very proud man. Plus his instinct was to protect Mum and do what was best for her which was far more important to him than my welfare at the time.

He also thought that if I did survive he would wrap me up in cotton wool and that would not be any good for me. The decision they made inevitably meant that the little imperfection which had come into their lives would be hidden away, and it certainly made their life easier. But I would not have liked to be in their shoes having to make it and I don't blame them for deciding the way they did.

It was said it would take about five weeks to find a place for me at a home for disabled children in Sussex called Chailey Heritage, but a place came available only after three weeks, two weeks early. Chailey's medical administrator, Dr E. P. Quibell, was a friend of Dr Evans. There were already over a dozen Thalidomiders living there, so they were not fazed by the challenge of me.

So five whole weeks after my mum had given birth, she travelled to Rochdale with my dad to see me for the first time. In his book my dad says that when they walked into the room I was covered up to the neck by a blanket and was being bottle fed by a nurse. They sat down beside the two of us and my mother paled when she caught sight of my flattened nose and pink birth mark. "Then the nurse drew back the blankets and Vicki saw the little flower-like limbs. She slumped against me and sobbed."

The long, sad journey they took from Lancashire to Sussex that day after my mother had recovered enough to face wrapping me up again and taking me in her arms has left me with what I believe to be my earliest memory.

Actually, it is not so much a proper memory as a warm, all-pervading feeling of being closely held, cuddled, loved and wanted. And then of the feeling suddenly changing to not being wanted and being left alone, cold and abandoned. This, I'm convinced, comes from when my mother laid me in a high-sided metal cot at Chailey and left me.

Though I know all the reasons they did it – the pressures, the lack of bonding, their youth and inexperience – and, as I've said, I don't blame them, I must confess that in the very bottom of my heart I have never really understood how they could give me, their own baby, away into care. After I gave birth to Emma, my feelings of love and commitment to her were so overwhelming, I understood it even less.

My mother has never spoken to me about what she went through on that day and I have only once asked her. It was soon after Dad began his campaign, I must have been nine years old and I remember shuffling into the kitchen and asking her something like, "How did you feel when I was born?"

She looked at me, really tearful and hurt, and I could see she wanted to say something. I was on the floor, I was her little girl – well, I was a girl on the floor that she had no real bond with – how could she tell me and lay the burden of what she really felt on me? I could see the pain and conflict in her eyes before she fled upstairs, really upset.

Dad went up to comfort her and when he came down we started talking about the campaign. He was telling me how Cliff Richard and Olivia Newton John would be coming to see me in a couple of days and the BBC would be filming it. Then Mum walked through the door and I changed the subject.

Years later my dad told me that he remembered that day and how I instinctively steered the conversation away from something my mum would find painful. So I don't know how she feels because I don't bring it up. All I know is that the one time I did, it was like she had been punched in the stomach.

Instead I protect her from being hurt. I think she's been hurt enough. None of it was her fault.

I have a good life and I don't feel bitter about the way I am; the only resentment I feel is that the scientists who created thalidomide and then did not give out the information they had about its side effects, especially in relation to unborn children, immediately it was known, deprived me of a loving childhood at home with my mother and father which has affected my life and relationships ever since.

Chapter Two
Life At Chailey

A FEW YEARS AGO I met up with my favourite nurse from Chailey, Miss Shepherd, who told me how she remembered me arriving that evening in the summer of 1962 "in your carry-cot, asleep, with tiny fair curls all over your head, looking like a sleeping angel. Your cot and covers were pretty and so were you. I fell for you on sight."

She also remembered how young and scared my parents looked, particularly my mother. "She was pretty, fashionable and well groomed but all of that was the outside. She was almost not there, the inner person. Her face was frozen and she hardly spoke. Your father behaved protectively towards her and did most of the talking. If you can picture her so, you will realise she was in a state of shock. But she was trying, poor girl, to come to terms with the tragedy that had happened to you, all three."

Chailey Heritage Hospital was founded in 1903 by a lady called Dame Grace Kimmins as an extension of her work with the Guild of the Poor Brave Things which she set up in 1894 to help disabled boys (or crippled, as they were called then) learn a craft and take a productive place in society.

She found a disused building in what she thought was a healthy, open air place near Lewes in East Sussex, and took 12 boys from London, mostly suffering or recovering from polio or TB. The idea was that the hospital would offer medical treatment and physical therapies, education and practical training all on the same site.

In 1948 it became an NHS hospital and over the years has become world famous for its approach to orthopaedics. The children were taught basic reading, writing and maths plus crafts like shoe-making, woodwork, basket-making and gardening.

When I arrived I joined about 22 other Thalidomiders, as we call ourselves, of which eight were four-limbs deficient like me while the others were mostly missing arms but not legs, and I was one of the youngest. The rest of the children at Chailey were suffering from the effects of all kinds of conditions such as polio, spina bifida, cerebral palsy, meningitis, Down's syndrome, congenital disorders, accidents or prematurity.

The hospital had a collection of those big Silver Cross sprung prams that looked like Citroens upside down and we must have been quite a sight when the nurses packed us Thalidomiders into them to take us for our afternoon walk. They used to sit us in them up to six at a time, two who hadn't got any legs but who had good balance like me would be plonked in the middle and two with legs would be put at either end. I don't remember them strapping us in but the sides were too high to jump out and they would tuck a blanket round us if it was chilly.

Across the road from Chailey there was a common while down the lane was a farm which belonged to the grandson of Sir Winston Churchill and there were picnic areas to left and right. We would be trundled off to the farm to see new baby chickens and a bottle-fed calf, down the lane to pick flowers in the hedges or for a wander through Warren Wood or to the common just to roll around on the grass.

Sometimes we would all go to Brighton for a day on the beach or to visit the Dolphinarium which would cause quite a stir. I remember once on a beach a woman near us muttered, "Such children should not be allowed out in public," but such hostility was rare. More often people would look disturbed, even upset, but sympathetic and compassionate too and some would thrust a £1 note into the nurse's hand saying "buy them all an ice cream" which, at that time, it would.

But we didn't think of ourselves as different. Or, at least, because everyone at Chailey was different, for us difference was normal. As I remember it, we were ordinary babies, admittedly without arms and legs but with all the initiative and mischievousness you could imagine. A lot of the other children needed medical care but we Thalidomiders generally didn't. We were robust and agile and we just got on with what we had got.

The ward for babies up to the age of 18 months was called PEC. Years later when I saw pictures of babies standing up in those high-sided cots in Romanian orphanages, it reminded me of those early years and the feeling of being in one of PEC's cots which were made of metal and cold to the touch.

It's not that I was neglected. All my needs were seen to: I would cry, then everyone else cried and the nurses would come and pick us up and take care of us. And I was never alone because there were always loads of people around.

It was just that there were so many of us and only four or five nurses so they didn't have the time or the energy to give each baby individual attention, so I grew up with the feeling of being alone in a crowd because I didn't have that special connection with one person.

Things were more formal then as well; the nurses were addressed by their titles, never their first names, and wore pale blue dresses with starched white aprons and caps and stout black shoes while the sister wore a royal blue dress with white removable puff sleeves, a high neck and a starched cap even taller than the nurses'. For outdoor wear they had navy blue capes, lined with red and fastened with crossed straps.

But underneath the uniform, Miss Shepherd was lovely. She was very small with glasses and curly hair going grey though she was still quite young. The most important thing was, however, that she had life in her eyes. For some nurses, working at Chailey was just a job but she was very maternal. She had a real vocation to look after the babies there and she also had a lot of compassion for the parents so she worked hard to make it as friendly and homely a place as possible for them to come and visit.

PEC was a long semi-circular dormitory with a corridor in front with 12-panel glass French doors to the outside. Grace

Kimmins had believed in doing everything in a military way and was a great believer in the health benefits of fresh air. So it was fresh air with everything: fresh air with exercise, fresh air when eating, fresh air when learning reading, writing and arithmetic, even fresh air when sleeping.

Most nights our cots were dragged on to the concrete play area outside – we only stayed indoors at night if it was actually raining, snowing, very windy or frosty but even then all the French doors were left open. If it was cold you were simply given extra blankets. As a consequence right up until my late twenties I couldn't stand central heating, finding it much too stuffy.

We got woken up at 6.45 a.m., changed, dressed and breakfasted at 7.30 a.m. As I got bigger and stronger I learned to get up by myself by turning on my front, wriggling up to the end of the bed, crawling up the headboard and bouncing my head off it to push myself up. The nurses used to watch me struggle, not out of cruelty but because the whole attitude at Chailey was to let you find out how to do things for yourself in order to push you into being independent.

My very earliest memory of life on PEC was one day when my best friend, Grahame Tindale, was messing around and Miss Shepherd picked him up and said, "If you don't shut up, I'll put you in the bin!" Then, as a joke, she plonked him in the wastepaper bin.

Until then we couldn't sit up on our own but when she put him in the bin she realised it was the ideal shape to keep him upright so she told the experimental Occupational Therapy workshop which used to make all kinds of aids for us. They adapted the idea and came up with a bucket-type seat, nicknamed a "flower pot", which we were sat in to strengthen our backs and improve our balance.

When we could sit up and shuffle or hop around, the nurses would lift us down to the floor in the morning and we would crawl to the bathroom where the ones that had legs would sit on little toilets and those that didn't sat on potties in rows.

The OT department made small frames to go round the

potties so we would waddle up, lean over one side and put a leg over, then lean over the other side to get up on the frame then shuffle on to the loo. When we'd finished we would call a nurse to clean us up then we'd waddle off to get dressed.

They taught us to dress ourselves with special sticks with an S shaped hook on the end. With that you could reach for a garment, get it over your head and with a bit of a wriggle it would come down. For doing up zips they put a length of tape attached to the zip-pull by a clip like you get on a dog lead. When I put my top on I made sure the tape came over my shoulder and was within reach, then I would lean against a wall for balance while I pulled on the tape to bring the zip up. Then I had to find a nurse to undo the clip.

Our toothbrushes and hairbrushes were attached to sticks so we could reach, though, in the case of brushing our hair, we couldn't apply enough pressure to get the knots out so everyone had to have short hair unless their parents objected. I remember there was one Spanish girl whose parents insisted that Spanish hair is always long so she was allowed to be an exception but she had to wear it up in a pony tail. To wash our hands they would fill the sink right to the top so we could reach the water and we each had flannels to wash our faces.

After we learned to sit up in our "flower pots", the OT department made us our first sets of artificial legs – I got mine when I was 17 months old. There was a bucket-shaped knickers contraption you sat in with two bits at the bottom with four feet coming out of them, one set going forwards, one going backwards so you couldn't fall over. In order to walk on them you had to lean from side to side.

None of us liked the legs. We were perfectly happy shuffling on our bottoms and we could get along really fast but in the mornings we were put in them to play with sand, water, paint, Playdoh, dolls, construction toys, dressing up and so on.

There were tables with half-moon shapes cut out of each side and we would stand in there and there would be a little gate that shut behind us to keep us upright. I used to like doing painting and things like that, like any other child, and I could manage all right. If there was something in the middle of the table I wanted, I would use something to reach it and pull it towards me.

We all held our pencils differently, finding a way depending what our fingers were like. Some had three fingers on one hand and four on the other, one or two people didn't have any on one arm. Those who had no arms at all would put a pencil in their mouths and draw with that, or if they had legs they might grasp the pencil with their toes.

We were quite happy to get on with things like that but the staff in the OT department loved making things "better" for us so they kept coming up with all sorts of funny contraptions to use for writing or drawing. One was a stick, shaped like a miniature crutch, with a piece at the top which was lodged in the armpit, two cross bars and a pencil attached to the end. We would hold on by either the first bar or the second bar and draw that way. Also the staff would tour the local toy shops looking for things we could manipulate with whatever we had for hands.

Often the staff would put something out of reach on the table, maybe a sweet or piece of fruit or something, and give us one of these aids to get hold of it. I found it much easier just to lie across the table and pick it up with my mouth but at Chailey a high degree of competitiveness was bred into us at a very early age. It was always: "Let's see who's going to be first" applied to everything – getting dressed, washed, finishing your dinner, trying anything new.

It gave me a real buzz to be the first to be able to do something so I'd try my best with all the contraptions they came up with to make us more "normal". And the more enthusiasm you put into something, the more likely you were to be given the next new thing.

Lunch was at about 12, then story time, sitting on the carpet. After lunch we were put down for a nap and I was often popped into a cot with Grahame, who was four-limbs deficient like me but 18 months older. I used to look up to him because he was older and stronger and we played together all the time – wherever Grahame went, I went. We just clicked, became best buddies, and grew up together like brother and sister.

In the afternoon from 2 p.m. to 3.30 p.m. we were divided into two groups for more formal activities like the beginning of reading, numbers and music. The rest of the time we played with the same curiosity and inventiveness of any toddler and because we were so small and really fast we would get into all sorts of little places and had to be pulled out of them.

We would hide underneath the hospital trolleys or wriggle into tiny gaps between the furniture and the wall or sit in a corner of the Wendy house with blankets over our heads. The playroom was full of little nooks and crannies where we thought we couldn't be found though the staff knew exactly where we were, I'm sure. Sometimes they would play a joke and leave me hiding when they put everyone else to bed and I'd suddenly realise I was on my own and scared and shout out, "I'm here!"

Babies stayed on PEC until they were about 18 months old and then moved on to Queen Elizabeth One ward in another building nearby, where we stayed until we were two and a half when we went to Queen Elizabeth Two until we were four and old enough to start full-time school.

QE One was similar to PEC in having lots of glass doors opening on to a big patio area. This play space was bounded by a wall in which there were three steps leading up to two paddling pools filled with two or three inches of water and a sandpit, all built with funds donated by the Friends of Chailey.

By the age of two we could crawl or shuffle along on our bottoms, swaying from left to right, or jump sideways to get along, and we could get over anything. I was particularly boisterous and tomboyish. I often toppled over but I could usually use the momentum to bounce off the floor straight back up again.

From about April on we would all pile into the paddling pools and splash around no matter how cold it was. As it got warmer we would roll around naked or with just a pair of knickers on. We didn't have to wear our artificial legs when playing so to get to the pools I would lie on the bottom step on my side, put one leg up then use my chin to haul up the rest of me. Sometimes a nurse would stand on the middle step and pop us up on the top one by one.

One of my favourite things was making mud pies so every opportunity I had to get to the sandpit would find me there making sandcastles with moats around. My right hand is quite strong so I could scoop up half a bucket of sand and fill it to the top with a spade, adding more sand and a bit of water and patting it down hard. Grahame and I made sandcastles together and I liked putting a lot of water in the moat. We usually finished by throwing mud at each other and getting into a terrible mess.

No matter how much fun I had with my friends, the best day of the week at Chailey for me until I was four years old was Sunday when either my mum and dad or nan and grandpa would come to see me. I also occasionally saw my other grandmother, my dad's mother, who had divorced and gone to live in Canada, my Auntie Di or my Auntie Hilary.

My other grandfather, my dad's father, would see me when I went home but also occasionally came to Chailey and that was special because he always took me to Chessington Zoo where I loved the penny arcade. He held me up while I put the penny in then he sat me on a table so I could pull the handle. We spent hours in there on 50p and I always came out with more than I started with which I was allowed to keep.

These visits were hugely important to me because, even though I didn't live with my family it meant I knew who they were, and therefore who I was. Some of the children saw their parents only rarely which meant they were lonely but at least had a semblance of a sense of identity but a few were completely abandoned. One child's parents lived only two and a half miles down the road but never paid a visit.

One of the former nurses told me that after a while the staff realised the thalidomide children needed more contact with their parents and set about encouraging it. "This was quite difficult as they had never had you as babies and so did not feel you really 'belonged'," she said. They had some success but there were also a number of divorces after a thalidomide child went home. The only time the abandoned children got out of

Chailey on their own was when they were taken on a day out by one of the Friends of Chailey.

On Sundays I went to church in the morning, had lunch, then a nurse dressed me in my best clothes and 2 p.m. would find me sitting waiting eagerly for my visitors with all the other excited children who were expecting visitors. Then Grandpa would walk through the door, my eyes would light up, his would light up, I would waddle over to him as fast as I could and he would pick me up, pop me on his hip, give me a big hug and say "Come on then," and off we would go.

My grandpa, Jack Whiteside, was very special to me because I felt he truly loved me for who I was. He was a big chap with dark hair and really kind eyes, a gentle giant a bit like the laid-back actor, Lee Marvin. He'd started as a trucker and built up his business through hard work and he was a strict Catholic. He treated me just like a normal kid, nothing to be frightened of, and he always used to tell me not to be frightened of doing anything, that I must try. Sometimes he used to pop in to see me unexpectedly on a week night on his way home when he had been fishing at Newhaven, which was a particular treat as it meant I got more than my fair share of visits.

My nan had been really pretty when she was young and was always happy, always smiling and very motherly. She came from a down to earth working-class northern family and spoke her mind but she also loved giving hugs and always stroked my head when she went past.

They drove for two and a half hours each way every other Sunday to take me out. We would go for a stroll on the common, picking wild strawberries in the summer. Often they would drive for another hour each way to take me for a ride on the Bluebell Railway or for a picnic on the beach at Newhaven or Brighton. Grandpa would spread the blanket out and Nan would get out the food. It was special, to be treated as if nothing was wrong.

Of course, the downside of having a lovely Sunday afternoon out was the pain of being left behind at Chailey at the end of it. I used to get upset when my grandparents left but not so much after my parents' visits because I could see the hurt in their eyes when they looked at me, particularly my mother's. It wasn't just her, all the Thalidomiders' parents had the same look in their eyes.

Sunday afternoons at Chailey after the visitors departed were hectic and highly emotional. Some children had had a grand time and would joyfully describe all the things they had done, others would cry, some would be nasty to the staff and some would be withdrawn, which is what happened to me.

All the little abandonments week after week took their toll and made me hard. I began to switch off in the last five or ten minutes of any visit and turn from a soft, loving child to a cold fish as a way of protecting myself. It didn't work completely, however, and the hurt would build up inside until every few weeks I'd explode and have an almighty argument or be really unpleasant to somebody, through nothing more than frustration. Every time a rejection happens, even now, I do the same. I go from happy and relaxed to tense and fierce; it's the wall I've built around my most sensitive feelings.

One Sunday in the summer that I became four years old I was surprised that Grandpa didn't come straight into the room where I was waiting when he arrived but went to see the ward sister first. I felt something was wrong and I heard the sister and the staff nurse whispering together but I didn't know what it was about. Then he picked me up but it wasn't happy and joyful as our meetings used to be. He was solemn.

He and my nan took me on to the common and spread the picnic blanket out. They had bought fresh strawberries from a farm on the way down and brought a bowl of sugar to dip them in. I adored strawberries so once I had eaten my sandwiches and a few of theirs, I'd forgotten my worries.

That was until Grandpa began to make the speech he had obviously been building up to. I remember so clearly how he was lying back on the blanket and I was jumping around on his stomach playing bouncey, bouncey, and Nan was saying softly, "Louise, you shouldn't do that to Grandpa," and then he turned to me and said, "Louise, this is going to be the last time we come here to take you out because I am not well."

I cried, "Oh no, you're fine, Grandpa. You can manage it, you're good, you're strong!" But in fact he had diseased kidneys, the travelling had become too hard for him and his doctor had told him he couldn't do it any more because he had to go on dialysis.

When he took me back to Chailey my brain knew he would not come again because he had told me but I didn't want to believe it and my heart would not accept it so I said what we always said when they left: "See you in two weeks!" He replied as gently as he could, "No, you won't," and left. Afterwards the sister came and told me again that Grandpa had said it was the last time, and because it came from her, it really hit home this time and I spent the evening crying.

The following Sunday it was my parents' turn to come. I remember less about their visits. I think we went out for drives or to a nearby tea shop where they were accustomed to Chailey children and a couple of times to the Bluebell Railway. I know that my mother got upset every time she came down and would cry on the way home.

I think I was in the car when they told me that they would not be coming again either because it wasn't fair on Nan to ask her to look after the rest of the family while she was caring for Grandpa on dialysis. By then my parents had two children besides me – the doctors had advised them to have another baby as soon as possible after my birth so they had had Claire 18 months after me, followed by David who was then a babe in arms.

I don't remember being too upset that my parents could not come again but I felt completely differently about Grandpa. When the next Sunday came I nagged and nagged at the nurses to dress me in my best clothes until they eventually consulted the sister and she said to put them on.

I sat there waiting with the other children as all their parents turned up and Grandpa didn't come. I really did think he was going to come until the last parent arrived and collected their child and there was still no sign of him and I was left on my own. I went and hid under a bed and fell asleep. I didn't come out until it was teatime and hunger drove me to it. I was extremely sad because then it really sank in that Grandpa had meant what he had said but I didn't talk to anyone about it. Instead I withdrew into myself.

I remember every Sunday after that how everyone else's parents would arrive one by one and I didn't have anyone. I felt lost. I didn't wait any more. I didn't bother to change. I went off with the other children who never had visitors and stayed in the ward or the play area until all the parents had gone away again. Then I would cry.

Chapter Three
Finding My Feet

WHEN I WAS FOUR I moved out of the pre-school accommodation and into the Junior Dorm, also known as St Martin's, along with all the other Thalidomiders except Andy who was not fit enough. He was later adopted by Mr and Mrs Wiles who changed his name to Terry and Mr Wiles wrote a book about their story called *On Giants' Shoulders*.

By then I was learning to be a real tomboy, a process which was greatly helped by the invention by the OT department of little trolleys on which we could get around as fast as we liked. They consisted of a wooden platform two or three inches off the floor with castor wheels at each corner for stability and wheelchair wheels attached to the sides which came up to your hand height and were set at an angle so you could push them round. We had races on them and used them as bumper cars. We were supposed to wear safety straps but I couldn't be bothered. I thought that, if I am going to fall out, so be it.

Grahame Tindale and I were great mates in those years. He came from a navy family and was a bit of a bossy type, a show-off, but because he was a year older I really did look up to him and we used to get up to so much mischief.

We were similar in disability so we learned from each other through play. We used to go on the swings together on our stomachs, shuffle up hills and roll down them again and go swimming together, bobbing about upright in the water like corks.

We played football sitting on the floor. We wore plastic spats on our feet, kicked the ball then shuffled after it on our bottoms. We often toppled over but we got so fit that if we rolled on our backs we could flip ourselves back up again. Sometimes we fell forwards and cut our chins or got stuck and had to find someone to climb on to get upright but we were much safer on the floor than on our artificial legs because we didn't have so far to fall.

I was always racing Grahame on our trolleys and we would see just how fast we could go. He was bigger than me and a boy so he always won. I had a bit of a rival called Lorraine Brasher who always wanted to play with Grahame as well. She was more girly girly and he had a bit of a soft spot for her while I was more of a buddy. She used to try to get in front of me to get nearer to Grahame but she was slower than me and, as I was a bit of a bully, I used to get there first and barge her out of the way.

We had a lot of freedom to go out on our own, much more than even able-bodied children get today. We went to the woods to play hide and seek or make dens or to the pond to dig up worms. We got about on our trolleys as far as they would go, then jumped off to scramble through the grass picking up caterpillars, snails, slugs or frogs.

In order to catch these fascinating creatures we inevitably got extremely dirty. In fact, we would come back absolutely caked in mud. Grahame went off to the boys' dorm where it was OK because that's what boys did but when I got back to the girls' dorm I'd find all the rest of them sitting there, colouring or doing embroidery like little princesses. So where they would have a bath every other day, I usually had one every single day, especially during the holidays.

The staff in Junior Dorm were much harder than the nurses in the babies' wards and one or two were downright nasty. They didn't care for us, just treated us as a job they had to do. At bathtime they used to scrub us with Pears soap and a brush and they were not soft brushes, your skin was red afterwards, and then they would really rub you dry. You know when you are cross with your kids and you dry them roughly and hastily: it was like that all the time.

They plonked you on the loo, then they might put your legs on with the straps too tight and when you complained would snap, "Oh, stop moaning," and would brush your hair really hard. Most of them had their favourites over whom they would spend more time which meant they would have to rush the others. But after Miss Shepherd I wasn't anyone's favourite because I wasn't the girly sort who sat around nicely playing with dolls.

I only had one use for dolls which came about because every summer I used to dehydrate so badly I ended up in hospital. We had drinks at certain times during the day: breakfast, break, lunch, tea and just before bed, and they were only little cups but we were running around and using up far more liquid than this. I was particularly badly affected because, unbeknown to me at the time, I had bad kidneys.

So every year they had to take me in and stick a needle in me to rehydrate me on a drip for two days. I would come out feeling pretty sore and sorry for myself so I would get hold of my doll and stick pretend needles in it, to act out the pain. I remember once my mum gave me a really posh doll with a porcelain face and pretty Victorian clothes. I didn't want it at all; I much preferred Action Man. So I stuck a few pins in it then threw it away.

It was easy to cover up doing something like that because most of the things that went to Chailey had to be shared and often went astray. If your parents brought biscuits, everyone had one; sweets, the same so that those who didn't have any parents visiting would have some. This was OK until it came to something you really, really loved, like my special party dress.

I didn't have a cupboard of my own for clothes. My clothes had my number sewn in – my number was 87 and it was on my shoes, my bed, my medical notes, everything about me – and put on a shelf in a big room. There were my Chailey clothes which I wore Monday to Friday, my home clothes which I wore on Saturdays and Sunday afternoons and my Sunday uniform for church.

My parents had given me this beautiful dress, royal blue with small, delicate red and gold flowers all over it. It was a typical 60s style, sleeveless with a round neck, tight bodice and a skirt that flared out so when I sat on the floor I could spread it around me and it was just as if I was sitting in water. It was gorgeous.

One day there was a birthday party; I was asked what I wanted to wear and I said "my beautiful blue dress", but when the nurse went to the shelf, it wasn't there. I was absolutely devastated but it was nowhere to be found so I had to wear something else. Then I went down to the party and somebody else had my dress on. She was a friend but the point was, the dress was mine. I was in floods of tears but I didn't get it back there and then. She carried on wearing it at the party then it was sent to the wash and put back on my shelf.

I became extremely protective over my clothes after that. I used to look in that cupboard every single day to make sure that dress was still there. For my play clothes of shorts and a T-shirt I would choose the most hideous colours like bright sunshine yellow shirt and blue shorts, or a red shirt with yellow stripes, something horribly loud so that nobody else would wear them.

This kind of thing taught me to be an individual very early on: growing up alone in a crowd makes you work out what you need, and fight for it. For instance, if you wanted some attention – and I craved it all the time – you basically had to shout for it or wangle it somehow.

Through needing help going to the loo, I began to realise that the best time for getting a one to one talk with a member of the staff when she wasn't busy doing something else was when I was on the toilet. So there I would sit for five or ten minutes, chatting away. I used to cherish those times.

School routine was like any other boarding school, apart from Chapel three times a week, Tuesday, Thursday and Sunday. There was a sort of uniform of zipped tunic tops and trousers and the food wasn't bad – Monday egg and chips, Tuesday some sort of stew, Wednesday roast, Thursday shepherds pie or stew from leftovers, Friday fish fingers and chips, Saturday sandwiches, Sunday roast.

In class we were put in our age groups and the emphasis was on reading, writing and arithmetic, that was all they were concerned with. I was in a class of about 12 children with all kinds of disabilities: three other Thalidomiders plus some Down's syndrome, some victims of road traffic accidents and others with cerebral palsy or spina bifida. We were not expected to do a lot.

As for learning how to cope with our disabilities, the approach was: look at what you need to do and work out how to solve the problem of doing it. So it was: OK, I need to get on that settee so how do I do it? Well, it could be by falling on it or jumping on it or crawling up it: they taught you not to be afraid of doing that kind of thing and to achieve what you could with what you'd got. This was good but it did lack individual care and nurturing. There was a distinct lack of love and cuddles.

We Thalidomiders were all perfectly happy propelling ourselves around on our little trolleys but Chailey insisted on fitting us with artificial legs almost as soon as we could walk. We were constantly being experimented on with artificial limbs. I believe their main aim was to try to make us look and move in as "normal" a manner as possible but I think it would have been better to have worked out what we could do with what we had got then to have devised aids to help us.

I got my first pair of legs at 17 months old and I got new ones made at the artificial limb centre at Roehampton in South West London every few months when I was small and growing fast, and later once a year. But I never felt comfortable or entirely safe and I wore my final pair for the very last time to walk down the aisle on my first wedding day.

I remember being in lessons when one of the nurses would come in and I would sit there thinking, who's next? Who is going to be pulled around this time? And dreading it being my turn, though if it was a lesson I didn't like, it was not so bad. Then they would call out a name and someone would have to go off to a leg fitting or to see the doctor.

I didn't mind going to see Dr Fletcher who was the one

who fitted my artificial legs because he was a nice gentleman with a kindly manner, but I hated going to the medical doctors because I felt like a guinea pig. For the regular ward rounds you had to sit on your bed while a whole crowd of people stared at you and discussed you: Dr Quibell, his secretary, the ward sister, your physiotherapist, your occupational therapist, the senior physiotherapist and occupational therapist, two medical doctors and perhaps a psychologist and a speech therapist. There was nothing wrong with me as far as I was concerned. I felt: I am as I am and I am not sick. On top of that, every new doctor who came to Chailey, whether as a member of staff or just on a visit, was curious to see what a Thalidomider was. Many of them came to do "case studies" on us, presumably as part of their research and, being four-limbs deficient, it was usually me or Grahame who had to go. We were always undressed by one of the nurses who sometimes left our knickers on, sometimes not, then we had to sit on the bed until the doctor came to poke and prod and pull at our limbs. No one ever asked our permission and every time it happened, I resented it a little more.

In contrast, I enjoyed going to the occupational therapists who had the task of trying to teach us to do things that a normal child would do or to find ways in which we could be independent with what we had got. They had a play house in the OT department and we spent happy hours in there playing house, sweeping up, ironing, pretending to cook and so on, while they watched to see how we tackled each task. Sometimes they left our artificial legs or arms on and other times they set us free to manage as we could.

I got to mess around in the play house while I was waiting to have the plaster cast made to fit my new artificial legs so they could get the buttock sockets right, which was the only pleasant part of an unpleasant and undignified process. Usually two of us went at a time and I would play until it was my time to go in. Then I would be stripped, slathered in Vaseline, encased in a Tubigrip suit and suspended from the shoulders an inch or two off the table. They put paper under my arms so the straps didn't cut into my armpits and hung me from a hoist like a piece of meat.

I was then wrapped from the waist down in a long cloth bandage soaked in heavy duty plaster which was clammy and cold until it began to warm up from my body heat. Each roll of bandage had a stick in the middle and, in the spirit of the usual Chailey rivalry, we used to compete with each other over how many sticks we came back with and what colour they were. I would hang there over the table for 15 to 20 minutes but the worst bit was when the scissors came out. They were sharp along one side and rounded on the other so they would not slice into you but occasionally, especially when I was maturing, they would catch a hair on my leg and really hurt. Despite the Vaseline which was supposed to stop the plaster sticking to me, I was always covered in bits after they took the cast off and had to be brushed down. The procedure was much the same for having a cast made for my artificial arms except that I could sit on the table or a chair instead of being hung in mid air.

From the cast they made a bucket shape out of leather that I sat in and put my legs through, with straps that went round my feet to hold the legs on. The technique was to lift from the waist, rock and kick. The legs were made from metal and stiff so I had to use crutches too but they had a knee lock which I operated with my hand so I could sit down.

When we were toddlers there were blue legs for girls and brown for boys and we also had stabilisers in front and behind. As I got older the legs were painted flesh colour. They had their advantages in that you could kick somebody and they could kick you back and you wouldn't feel anything and they made you the same height as everyone else so you could get eye-to-eye contact. They were good for slow dancing as a teenager, though I always used to tread on people's toes without realising, and they were the only way I could stay on when horse riding, which I used to love.

But it always felt like walking on stilts with no arms to protect myself if I fell over. I used to wear a protective hat and call out to whoever came near, "Don't knock me over!" When I fell, I fell flat like a blackboard and I was forever doing it and hurting myself quite badly. I can't count how many times I cut open either the back of my head or my chin. I used my crutches because I felt more secure that way though I could walk without them and I had perfected a way of jumping through them to get along faster. One day I was coming down a ramp and I slipped and fell down and sliced my chin open, again the next day I went down the ramp and round the corner and slipped again and cracked my head open.

I was forever up in the sick bay getting stitched up. I remember one of the last times I fell over I had gone past the science lab and I slipped, cut my chin and swore. That time, as well as the stitches, I got a detention for swearing. I fell so many times on my chin that it caused a great big dent and I had to have plastic surgery to fill it up. You can still see the scars today.

At least the legs had some advantages but when they decided to fit us with artificial arms, the fun went out of playing. We used to get along fine launching ourselves across the table to reach something and throwing things to each other, maybe not very accurately but quickly and efficiently, but with the arms on we were always forced laboriously to stretch them out get hold of something or pass it to someone else which was slow, cumbersome and boring.

The first set of arms had elbows with elastic band type strings which were attached to a frame shaped round your body like a waistcoat and which you pulled with your hands to manipulate. Later on, when I was eight or nine, I was fitted with Hendon arms which were hydraulic and worked on a mixture of gas and water. They weighed a ton. A gas cylinder was strapped to my back then there was a harness-type jacket made out of some carbon fibre that went over my shoulders and clipped in the middle. These two heavy arms that weighed a stone together were fixed to the harness and I had a set of switches near my right and left hands to operate them. We were taught how to feed ourselves with them, how to write and even how to cook.

We had to wear the legs from 7.30 in the morning until 4 in the afternoon on a school day and from 7.30 until 12 on a

Sunday. The arms were worn for some classes and some lunches. Saturdays we didn't have to wear them at all. We all became quite professional at using them but none of us liked wearing them and not just because of the weight. When we had our legs and our arms on we looked like Robocop (or in today's terms, Transformers). But the arms would dig into me, every time I moved my hand I heard "hss, hss" from the gas and water power system and they were forever going wrong. I felt more disabled in them than I did without.

The only good use for them was when we had to eat lunch. Messing around with the gas and water would make them very jiggy so if you put peas or something sloppy on your fork and waited for a teacher or warden to pass and you jigged your arms the food would fly off the fork and hit them. It was really funny because you just had to say it was the arms and that they couldn't do anything about it.

The first thing we all did at 4 p.m. when we came in from school was to take our arms and legs off as fast as possible. It was that feeling of *freedom*, like kicking your shoes off at the end of a day at the office. We would put our play clothes on and go out to roll about in the fields or to play football. I would go and visit my growing collection of pet animals.

We would use our little trolleys or a few had wheelchairs when they got a bit older. Grahame stopped using his legs at about 12 and for some reason was let off and allowed to use a wheelchair. He realised his crutches were the same height as the chair so he started using them like paddles to push himself along and we would run around together.

Junior Dorm was run very much like a junior boarding school by Sister Myers who was strict but grandmotherly. There were fewer visits from doctors as you had to be medically fit and able to walk to go there and we slept indoors. A bell rang for morning call at 7.30 a.m. then it was get up, dress, put legs on, breakfast bell at 8 a.m., teeth clean, make bed and school at 9 a.m. Back from school at 4.15 p.m., legs off, tea 4.45 p.m., watch TV, play until 6 p.m. and bed at 9 p.m.

After my parents and grandparents stopped coming to visit

me at Chailey, I went home for visits three times a year for a week at a time at Christmas, Easter and the summer holidays. Every time I went home and was sent back to Chailey at the end of the week, it would kill me. Every single time. When I was about six, one of the former nurses recalls me saying, "Three weeks in the year, that's not very long to go home is it? Why?" and she told me that, unlike staff at Chailey, my parents had no experience of disabled and were so shocked when I was born they felt unable to look after me themselves. She told me how much they wanted a baby and how much they loved me and how guilty they felt. So I said, "I shall write to Mummy and tell her it wasn't her fault; it was the fault of the doctor who gave her the tablets."

But up until I was seven, my visits home were joyful. Mum or Dad would come and get me in the car and take me to the big house we had in Totteridge, North London. I would walk as we had to wear our legs to go home in. The legs came off, then I went into the kitchen where Mum would lift me up and put me on the kitchen table or a chair. I would sit there, gazing at her, drinking her in. There was always an au pair who did the housework and maybe got the tea ready, but Mum would look after me and I loved having her bath me and dress me, brush my hair and tuck me up in bed, enjoying those little intimate things the more intensely because it happened only on those short visits.

My parents were advised to have another baby as soon as possible after they put me in Chailey and my sister Claire was born just over a year after me. I think she was what my mum needed and I was not made to feel that I had been replaced by the perfect specimen. My grandpa didn't allow that to happen. He and my dad made sure whenever I went home that I was treated as the eldest. I'm afraid it put my sister's nose out a little because, when I wasn't there, she was the one who was last to go to bed and could sit at dining table when the younger kids had to sit in the kitchen. But when I came home, she had to go in the kitchen or everyone was allowed in the dining room. At the same time I resented her a little because she would get better quality toys because I was taking mine back to

Chailey where they were likely to get lost or damaged and she would get nicer clothes as it didn't matter if we had nice clothes at Chailey.

Though I loved being at home, I hated and dreaded the two-hour journey there and back as I suffered from terrible car sickness. Chailey's solution to car sickness was to forbid you to have breakfast before the journey which made things a lot worse. When I hadn't eaten since 4.30 p.m. the day before and my parents came to get me at 10 a.m., I was really, really hungry and when kids get over-hungry, they get sick and with my stomach empty, what I would bring up was bile. They came armed with lots of paper bags and I spent the whole journey puking up in the back of the car.

The smoother the car, the worse it got. On one occasion when I was 9 or 10 and the compensation battle was going on, my dad had just got a brand new Rolls Royce which he was extremely pleased with. I was really proud he was coming for me, this posh man in a posh suit whom everyone looked up to, oh yes, David Mason; no, David Mason; three bags full, David Mason. He was like royalty. I was dressed in a new blue poncho and was wearing my legs because you had to when you left Chailey and I felt pretty special as he signed me out and ushered me out to his gorgeous new car. I said, "Wow, that's a really nice car!" It had a fantastic smell of new leather, it was out of this world. I was helped into the car, with my legs on, it was so comfortable, and then he drove off. I was used to a little rickety coach or minibus from Chailey which rocked from side to side but this was a completely smooth motion and I felt sick as soon as the wheels started turning – I didn't know the trick that you have to look at the clouds.

We had gone about three miles up the road and I thought, ooh, I don't feel well! But then I thought, no, I cannot be sick in Dad's new Rolls Royce. I'm going to keep it in. So I asked him to open the windows a bit. He could see me changing colour, going from pink to pale to white to pale green to green. He said, "You are not going to be sick, are you?" I groaned "no" then promptly puked up all over his new car. He was furious because he had convinced himself I wouldn't be sick in his car, he thought it was my mum's driving. When we arrived home he got me out of the car and said, "Louise has been sick again, all over my new car." I felt so embarrassed. I was crying because Dad was angry, he was fuming because I'd been sick all over his car and Mum was frantic because we'd just got a new nurse in. They carried me upstairs and changed my clothes and when I came down I could hear my dad still going on to Grandpa: "That brand new car! I only picked it up yesterday.." etc. But my nan, who also suffered from car sickness, whispered to me, "Don't worry about it," which made me feel a bit better. Even now I still get car sick. The last time I went in a Rolls Royce was when my daughter, Emma, was born and my husband, John, had booked one to bring us back home. It was only a mile and half from the hospital and I felt sick all the way. It's not the leather smell but the smoothness of the car. A Rolls Royce looks nice and I'm sure it is a really smart car but I'd much rather choose a rickety old jalopy than a smooth luxury saloon.

During my visits home, I shared a room with my sister, Claire, though I never saw much of her because she seemed to be always out riding or taking care of her horse. I was really close to my brother, David, who has always treated me like a normal person. We played a lot together and, as she got a bit older, my younger sister, Lindsey, would join in. My parents wanted to make it a special week for me and we would play games, like Monopoly or backgammon, do painting, watch a lot of TV in the study, go out for a walk, visit my grandparents or they would come over.

Sometimes I thought, this is boring, spending all day in the house playing games. It was nice but not what I called a full life but then I thought this must be what normal families did. Years later I found out it wasn't normal at all when I overheard David telling one of his friends on the phone that he couldn't come out because I was at home. I asked him why he couldn't go and he said, "Because Mum and Dad say I've got to stay here otherwise you would be on your own."

One Christmas Eve we went to bed early. I was sleeping on a put-u-up in Claire's room and Mum tucked me in but I woke up about 2 a.m. It was always me who would wake up and say to Claire: "Are you awake?" She said "No," but I was so excited about Father Christmas that I wouldn't let her go back to sleep. I said, "Oh look, Claire, look at the bottom of your bed!" There were great big pillow cases full of toys. I whispered, "Go and wake David up to see if he's got his." So David came in with his presents and we all set about opening them. Claire decided to sit on the end of my bed and because she was heavier than I was, her weight pressed it down and I got flipped out of bed. All of us collapsed, laughing. I managed to put my top half on the bed and Claire lifted my legs and chucked the rest of me on, which meant I bounced and the bed folded, by which time Mum came along saying, "What's all the noise? Is that you, Louise?"

I was always getting in to trouble and getting a telling off. To my brother and sisters, getting a ticking off from my parents was serious and it devastated them. But because Chailey used the cane, being called a bad girl was nothing and didn't have any effect on me. My dad put the bed back together again and put me in it and said sternly, "You're not allowed to open these until it's light." He opened the curtains slightly and it was eight in the morning before it was light again but we waited obediently and only came downstairs after we'd eaten all the chocolate.

To get downstairs I would lie on my front and bump down so that my bum would go first, then I would crawl on my bum from the bottom of the stairs to the kitchen and my mum would pick me up and put me on the chair. After breakfast, David and Claire would go off to do what they were doing. I might do drawing but mostly I would just sit there and watch my mother. She would take me off the kitchen table to wipe it down and then I would sit on the floor, but nothing would move me from her side or my eyes from her as she went about her ordinary everyday routine.

At bedtime, I would waddle into the lounge to find my father sitting in his favourite chair. Each of us go would go up in turn to say goodnight and give him and Mum a kiss. I would be lifted on my dad's lap for a couple of minutes for a hug, then Mum would put me on her hip, carry me upstairs and put me to bed. It doesn't sound much but these little routines were so precious to me. I was only home for seven days and most of one of them was spent getting there and another getting back so there wasn't much time to savour the little contact I had with my parents.

And the day before I went back was spoiled because I used to get so upset at the thought of having to leave the next day. I'd start getting upset as I packed my bag the day before I left, then on the day I would have to say goodbye to Claire, David and Lindsey, when I didn't want to leave them and I'd inevitably be sick on the way back to Chailey. However, no matter how terrible I felt, I didn't cry. Instead, I became withdrawn.

Usually my mum took me back, my friends would be waiting for me and I was very glad to see them. My mum would find the nursing sister, say, "Here's Louise's suitcase," then say goodbye and I would watch her drive away, feeling very alone. It was like that feeling after a holiday in a hotel which has been all grandeur and luxury and everything done for you and you get home and think, oh God, look at all the dust, no one's done the dusting. You come back down to earth. It was that feeling, going from luxury and love to fending for oneself and the basics. I had connections with friends, but no connection with family. In fairytales, TV shows and films for children, the mum and dad were always at the heart of the story, more so then than now. Mine were not at the heart of my life and it meant I always felt like I was on my own in a crowd.

As I got older, I inevitably grew more jealous of my sisters and brother, but also in a way I wasn't because I recognised that my dad is a control freak. So where I could do what I wanted, within the boundaries set by Chailey, I realised that my brother and sisters could not and that I had considerably more freedom than they did. We had a tuck shop trolley every day when I was in junior dorm. My parents would send 10p a week – it was a fortune! I could get a packet of crisps for two and a half pence, chocolates at two for a penny or wine gums in snake shapes at four for a penny. So I would get seven pence worth of those, plus a packet of crisps and maybe a lollipop that would be my sweets for the week. My grandpa used to send a packet of Penguin biscuits every Monday as well. So I had sweets every day when the children's programmes were on TV and I knew that David, Claire and Lindsey didn't.

Also, living in an institution, I could pick and choose my friends and change them at will. If I didn't want to say hello to somebody in the morning, I didn't have to, but my brother only had my sisters and they only had him and they all had to respect my mum and dad. If I didn't want to sit with someone at breakfast, I didn't have to. I could go and sit with someone else. People often ask me if I envied them but in this respect, I didn't, because I liked the freedom of knowing that if I didn't get on with someone or I had an argument, I could just choose someone else to be with.

I was a tomboy, mischievous and naughty a lot of the time at Chailey, and I was just the same when I went on my visits home. One day this led to one of the unhappiest incidents of my childhood. It was when David was about five and he and I started rolling around together on the floor in the study. We were just messing about and having fun but by accident he pulled my foot back which hurt. Looking back on it, I think he was trying to straighten my leg. At Chailey if you didn't shout loudly and the care staff didn't hear you, then you could get badly pulled around and bullied. So I knew how to yell if someone hurt me, and I really yelled.

Hearing me shrieking, my mum understandably thought I had been seriously hurt and she came flying down the stairs in a panic, got hold of David by the collar, smacked him – which was something she never normally did – for hurting me and fled back up the stairs crying. Feeling very upset, David ran after her to say sorry but got to her just as she had stormed into her bedroom and was slamming the door and she accidentally shut it on his fingers.

Just then Claire came in from riding to find David screaming and with his fingers blown up like balloons, Mum in the bedroom, crying, and me cowering under the stairs frightened because I didn't know exactly what was going on. She rang my dad and told him what had happened and he came back from work and left me in the house with the au pair while he took David and my mum to hospital to have David's fingers seen to. When they came back Mum went upstairs, still very upset, and David, who had been sedated to have his fingers plastered up, went to lie down. Meanwhile the au-pair had packed my bags and my dad took me straight back to Chailey.

I had only been home a few days, not the whole week, and being packed off to Chailey made me feel that the whole drama was all my fault. From that day on my mother never did anything physically for me again. Never bathed me or dressed me, brushed my hair or tucked me up in bed. She didn't feel she could cope any more. Instead she hired a nurse to look after me for my three weeks holiday a year so though I still spent the time at home, it didn't feel like home. I didn't resent having nurses at Chailey because that was what Chailey was. They were always changing so you constantly had strangers looking after you but it was water off a duck's back after a time. But I did resent having nurses at home, very much, so I used to play up. I thought that if David and I played up enough, the nurse would go, so we would do some really rotten things. My mother always had to warn them before they came: "Louise is very lively and will play tricks on you."

A favourite was to make the nurse an apple pie bed, which I had learned to do at Chailey. That's when you pull the bottom sheet up and fold it over the top so when the person gets in they can't get their feet more than half way down the bed. Then we would put pine cones and worms under the pillow. One nurse was an old lady, very regimental and protective, making us go out for an afternoon walk every day. David was ordered always to hold on to my wheelchair but one day I told him to let go at the top of a slope and I pushed myself along very fast with my crutches. I knew I could control myself but the nurse didn't and I went flying down the slope with her chasing after me. When she got us home she was in tears. Later that night she told Dad that she was leaving. Dad persuaded her to stay as there were only three days to go until I went back to Chailey.

I didn't get many kisses and cuddles as I was growing up. I would get a kiss goodnight from my mum and dad as I was on my way upstairs when I was home and I sat on my dad's lap occasionally until I got too old, but that's all. I wanted cuddles but, because I couldn't give them, people didn't realise. Whatever mood they are in, people express themselves so much with their legs and arms and they also read other people's body language subconsciously. If you've got no arms or legs, your body language is not the same and you can only express yourself with your face and your eyes. You can't run up to somebody and give them a cuddle, you have always got to wait for them to do it. It is something that has affected all my relationships.

I read many interviews in the papers about how other Thalidomiders' mothers felt, about how depressed they were after their children's birth. It's the sort of thing you don't necessarily believe when you see it written once but when you read it over and over again, you think it must be true and you wonder, is this what my mum thinks? And I could see the hurt in her eyes every time she looked at me. I remember once watching David coming up to her, and then Lindsey, and her looking at them calmly and then I came along, and all she wanted was to turn away.

I don't blame her. I could see the anguish she was going through because I could never be the daughter she wanted. Physically, that is. Mentally, I never got the chance. It wasn't just her. The same look was in the eyes of all the parents who came to Chailey. It was guilt and hurt. And in a strange way it was almost as if I became the adult in our relationship because I felt I wanted to protect her from those painful feelings.

Nowadays parents are encouraged and helped to look after their disabled children at home. Residential institutions still exist but generally have weekly boarders and all the children are encouraged to keep up their family life. Whether my parents were right or wrong to put me in Chailey is up to them and their consciences but it means that I grew up feeling towards them as I might towards houseparents. I don't know them that well. At the same time, I have always been able to recognise that there are things which bind us. There are things they do which I do, likes and dislikes that we share, which cannot come from watching them or being with them, it must be in the genes. So I know them in the sense that what I'm like, they are like, but to my eternal regret, I don't know them in the sense that my children, Emma and Jack, know me.

Understanding the reasons why things happened the way they did in my childhood brings forgiveness, but it doesn't stop the hurt. Over the years I developed what I think of as a little cupboard inside me where I put all my hurt emotions in. So something hurts, I cry, I store it away and that's it. I close the door and don't look inside again. The memories don't go away and occasionally the door swings open slightly and I remember the hurt. But as soon as I realise what's happened, I shut the door firmly again because I know that I've been hurt too many times to be able to risk letting all those memories come tumbling out.

Chapter Four
My Dad's Fight For Compensation

My father's courageous, determined, single-minded fight for adequate compensation for the thalidomide children from the Distillers Company made him very well known in the early 70s. He was always on TV or in the newspapers and I was often photographed too.

I was five years old in February, 1968 when the 62 sets of parents of thalidomide children who had brought negligence actions against Distillers received an offer of compensation of £15,000 each, which was reckoned to be 40% of what a court would have awarded if it had found against the company.

My father was incensed at how pathetic the award was for people who might never be able to earn their own living, and even more enraged because I and the rest of the thalidomide children were excluded from the settlement offer because our parents had not sued within three years of the damage being done and were therefore "time barred".

So the first thing he did was to apply to court for permission to issue a writ against Distillers "out of time". His lawyer said there was a loophole in the law and he thought he had a case because I had never lived with my parents and was therefore not in the "best position", as legalese put it, to get their advice on matters of law. This application was granted but the lawyer still thought there was very little chance of winning a case for negligence against Distillers in court and he advised the parents instead to get together and negotiate a settlement for everybody.

Arguments went on behind the scenes until November, 1971 when a new offer arrived from Distillers. They said they would set up a charitable trust of £3,750,000 for the children left out of the first offer, an average of about £8,000 each, plus pay £1,500 to each set of parents.

But there were strict conditions – the offer must not be made public and it must be accepted by every parent. If only one turned it down, the entire sum would be withdrawn and nobody would get a penny.

Knowing what happened in the end and looking back from today's culture of huge compensation settlements being a regular occurrence, this initial offer looks scandalously puny. But to most of the parents who had already been struggling to cope with their thalidomide children for ten years and who were being told by their lawyers they had no chance of winning in court, it looked like good money.

A big meeting was held in London, attended by about five hundred people, where the offer was spelled out. At the end all the parents dutifully lined up to sign the forms accepting the offer except my dad who stormed out in a rage. At other meetings round the country all the parents signed too. The result was that my dad was told he was the only one holding out and was therefore preventing everyone else getting their settlements.

It was at that point that he decided to harness the power of the press. A friend introduced him to the editor of the *Daily Mail*, the late David English (later to become Sir David) who ran the story over two pages on December 20, 1971 under the headline "My Fight for Justice – by the Father of Heartbreak Girl Louise." It was a brave thing to do – none of the other papers ran the story because their lawyers had warned their editors that it could lead to them being accused of contempt of court.

Meanwhile the lawyers acting for the other parents tried another tactic. In March, 1972 my dad was served with a writ for his removal from his office as Next Friend of Louise Mason – the Next Friend being the person entitled to take legal action on behalf of a child under 18.

The argument was that, because my dad was refusing Distillers' offer and so risking getting no compensation at all, he was not acting in my best interests. Another parent of a thalidomide child, Kenneth Arthur Taylor, had volunteered to take his place and become Special Next Friend of Louise. In other words, I would be made a ward of court.

Dad got to work phoning as many thalidomide parents as he could find and eventually discovered there were four others who had either not signed the acceptance form or regretted doing so and who had also been served with writs to have their Next Friend status removed. When the case went to the High Court of Justice it was decided the judge would rule on Dad and his decision would then apply to all five couples.

Dad lost the case but his lawyers lodged an immediate appeal. In the Appeal Court the three distinguished judges headed by Lord Denning reversed the decision of the lower court, unanimously agreed that my father's attitude was completely reasonable and said he could continue as Next Friend to fight for my interests.

This is the account given in my father's book and I have no reason to doubt it. Except for one strange thing – I have been told for as long as I can remember that I WAS, in fact, made a ward of court and that was the reason I was not allowed to go home for two years, which is a very long time when you are nine and ten years old.

However, I later realised that the first Christmas I was left on my own at Chailey was 1971, three months before my father was served with the writ. I remember the ward sister of Junior Dorm breaking the news to me as gently as she could but I didn't really believe her. I thought, oh, my mum and dad will come and get me. They won't leave me for Christmas. As a child you can't bear to think your mum and dad don't want you home.

There were nearly 100 children in Junior Dorm and on Christmas Eve everybody was collected one by one until there was only one other kid with me. Then she went home and I felt completely unwanted. I think I hid under the table. The four or five nurses and the sister on duty were all impatient, wanting to get home too, but they couldn't leave because I was still there.

So one of the nurses, who was called Janice, asked the sister if she could take me home and, once they had got permission from my parents, she took me for two nights to her house in Eastbourne where she lived with her parents and brother. I remember her carrying me in and sitting me on the bar they had in the living room and her telling me jokingly that I was not to drink.

Another thing that happened before the writ was that I had had to go to hospital for an operation on my nose around my ninth birthday in June, 1971 and my parents didn't even visit. I had no bridge to my nose which meant the hairs irritated the inside of it, causing it to stream as if I had a continual cold. If I did have a cold, I got into a horrible yucky mess so they decided to send me to the Ear, Nose and Throat Department at Guys Hospital in London, just a mile away from my dad's gallery.

The sister at Chailey asked my parents if they would like to have me home for the weekend and then take me to hospital on the Monday morning but my parents said they were unable to do this, so a nurse took me there two days before my birthday, put me to bed, said, "Be good, see you in a couple of days," and left me. I remember being very frightened because I'd never been away from Chailey except to go home, I didn't know anyone and the hospital staff didn't know how to cope with me. I didn't like doctors at the best of times and I hated being prodded and poked so I was really miserable.

As I was being prepared for the operation there was an emergency: the Queen Mother got a chicken bone stuck in her throat, so I was postponed. She came first. The next day they took me to theatre and drilled a hole in the roof of my mouth through which they inserted a plastic bridge.

I woke up in a ward in Great Ormond Street Children's Hospital with a "nose bag" on – string going over my ears from which a piece of gauze was suspended under my nose, like a white moustache. When they gave me a cup of tea, they gave me a full cup and an empty cup. As I drank the tea half of it went up the hole and out down my nose and I had to catch it in the empty cup. It was dreadful.

On the fourth day I was there one of the physiotherapists from Chailey, Miss Spears, who was also my Girl Guide leader, came to visit and I was so pleased to see her. She brought me some lovely smelling talcum powder and spent two or three hours with me. The only trouble was that when she left I felt even more lonely and abandoned. I always hoped I would wake up and find my parents had come but they never did.

The next day I went back to Chailey, still with the nose bag on. The one full, one empty cup business went on for another two weeks, then it mostly healed over though I still find drink coming out of my nose if I am not careful as it never completely sealed.

It may be that my parents didn't want me in the holidays because they were just too frantically busy, my dad with the campaign and my mum with helping to look after Grandpa who was by then very seriously ill with kidney failure.

Dialysis machines were new and rare at the time, especially at home, but my family had bought one and my nan, mum and aunt had trained to use it. Every time Grandpa was on it, someone had to sit with him in case something went wrong, and afterwards everything had to be thoroughly cleaned and sterilized. So Mum was spending hours there, taking her turn, at the same time as having three children under eight to look after.

From reading my medical records I also discovered that my parents were advised not to have any more contact with me because I was getting so dreadfully upset every time I went home. I was very distressed by the confusion of being made a fuss of at home where I was treated as number one, then being sent back to Chailey and having no more contact except a phone call once a week.

Then there had been the incident when David hurt my foot. So I guess a lot of things just added up. At the time, of course, I was not so understanding; in fact I thought I was getting a really raw deal. Every Christmas and birthday during those two years my mum would ring up and say: "What do you want?" and I would say: "I want to come home." That's all I would say: "I want to come home, just come home."

No one who read all the stories in the papers and magazines or watched me on TV programmes like the BBC's Nationwide could have guessed how miserable I was because in every photo I was smiling, looking like a happy little girl. There were pictures of Louise riding a horse and of Louise and her mum and dad but the papers never actually said I only went home three weeks of the year. I am sure everyone reading those stories must have assumed that I was being brought up at home and this was normal life for me. And I was actually genuinely happy for the ten minutes it took to take the pictures. I was happy because I was sitting on a bench with my family around me.

Most of the photographs were actually taken at my Auntie Di's house in Surrey, which was closer to Chailey than my parents'. Lots of the other thalidomide families thought I was being brought up at home as well because they saw pictures in magazines of Louise on a horse or Louise with dogs, without realizing that it was my aunt's horse and dogs. On one occasion when my dad and I were on Nationwide, he was in London and I was in a studio somewhere else with my aunt. It looked as though we were talking to each other but it was actually via a TV screen.

All the fuss was exciting for me and I was spoiled rotten too, especially when I went to TV studios with my dad. I loved going in the green room to meet the other guests before we went on and having make-up put on. They always put so much make-up on it felt like paste plastered over your face but it's because you have to be more colourful to look normal for the camera.

I met pop singer Rod Stewart, the hugely popular Australian singer, Olivia Newton John, the Welsh football player and manager, Mike England and singer, Cliff Richard (now Sir Cliff) of whom I have very fond memories as he was so friendly. While the others bent towards me with their hands on their knees to say hello – I was on the floor as I didn't have a wheelchair then – Cliff sat down next to me, crossed his legs and spoke face to face to me. The BBC were filming us and told me not to look at the camera. Cliff asked, "Can you count?" and "Have you seen any of my films?"

As soon as the photographers went away, I was taken straight back to Chailey where I was very fond of pointing to people on the television and telling the other kids: "I've met him or her." At first they were interested and excited too but when they found out about what my dad was doing, things began to turn nasty.

They saw the pictures of my parents' big house and accused me of being posh and snobbish. They started prodding and poking at me saying: "Oh, she thinks she's superior," and "Who do you think you are?" After they discovered my dad was holding out on the compensation they said things like: "It's all right for you, your dad's rich. I live in a two up, two down, with no central heating. I have no clothes except for what Chailey gives me. When I go home, I've got nothing."

I could see where they were coming from. The offer was a lot of money in those days. I didn't know what to say to them. They told me to talk to my dad and tell him to sign, and I would get on the phone to them and start chatting about it but then I would think, no, I can't do this. My loyalty was to my family, despite everything, and I was proud of what my father was doing. All I could say to the other kids was: "It's nothing to do with me," but they would come back with: "You're his daughter."

What hurt most was that the person who turned against me the fiercest was my best buddy, Grahame Tindale, not because we had fallen out, but because our fathers did.

In fact, a real hatred grew up between his dad and mine and one day they clashed dramatically on the Nationwide programme when my dad accused Grahame's father of having "a 24-inch mouth". This was splashed all over the newspapers which were delivered every day to the library at Chailey. The next morning Grahame went in there and read it, then someone came running out telling everyone about it and taunting Grahame: "Your dad has got a 24-inch mouth." So Grahame turned to me and said to me, "Well, your dad has got a 48-inch mouth."

Because he was older than me, Grahame had lots of people backing him up and not just Thalidomiders. There was some resentment against the Thalidomiders anyway because we knew what had caused our disability while a lot of the others didn't. There were plenty of crazy theories around, such as that eating green potato skins in pregnancy caused the baby to have spina bifida, but only we knew for certain that we were as we were because our mothers had taken Distaval.

The result was the rest of them ganged up on me. They made snidey remarks behind my back, tried to trip me up sometimes and finally sent me to Coventry. I went through a period of about eight months when I didn't talk to anyone except for brief conversations in class. In the playground and after school, I was totally alienated.

I went from being a popular, bouncy, you couldn't keep her down type person who was probably pretty arrogant to someone who was shunned. For my part, I couldn't stand any more bickering and reacted by withdrawing into myself and keeping my head down. I didn't trust anyone, all the people I thought were my friends had turned on me because of something my dad had said, not me.

However, I've always had a capacity for seeking out love. If it is turned off from one source, I go looking until I find it from another. So when all my friends stopped talking to me, I turned to animals who never let me down or hurt me. Instead they gave me love and attention and they needed me. Animals, especially my beloved dogs, have been a huge and constant source of comfort to me ever since that time.

It started when the school let me look after the laboratory hamster in the holidays. Then they let me have a fish tank where I gradually accumulated 33 goldfish. Over the next few years my menagerie grew to include a rabbit called Bungo, some newts and a snake and in the summer holidays I looked after everyone else's hamsters when they went home, about 12 of them.

Meanwhile my dad was turning into an internationally known figure after he won the powerful support of *The Sunday*

Times. The then editor, Harold Evans, began one of the most effective campaigns in newspaper history on September 24, 1972 with a story headlined: "Our Thalidomide Children: A Cause for National Shame." The deaf Labour MP, Jack Ashley, also got involved and introduced a motion in the House of Commons in November, 1972 calling for Distillers to face up to their moral responsibilities.

There was more publicity when lots of Distillers' shareholders came in on Dad's side and the whole campaign gathered pace. The American consumers' champion, Ralph Nader, even offered to support a boycott of the company's products. Distillers increased their offer to £5 million, plus £2,500 for each set of parents, on the eve of the parliamentary debate. Later they upped it to £20 million to be paid into a charitable trust over ten years, plus £5000 for the parents. Yet still my dad held out.

His tenacity was rewarded when on April 14, 1973, a month before my 11th birthday, Distillers finally came up with an offer which my dad approved. It was a cash payment of £6.8 million to the parents, plus £2 million a year for seven years to be paid into a charitable trust. And the annual payments were to be protected against inflation by up to 10 per cent which was thought likely to add another £6 million, bringing the total compensation up to £26 million.

That night Dad went on the television news on both BBC and ITN to say his fight was at an end (though, being Dad, he still had a couple of conditions he wanted Distillers to meet). It was the Easter holidays and I had been transferred from junior dorm to Rennie Ward to be with the other children left at Chailey for the break.

At 6 p.m. the news came on the TV and I saw my father so I started shouting excitedly, "It's my dad, my dad!" and everyone else joined in, yelling, "Oh Louise, there's your dad!" and I couldn't hear a word he said.

So I went to the sister and said to her my dad was on TV and I couldn't hear a word and I said to her, "Can I stay up until 9 p.m. to see the news again?" and she said "Yes." Because I hadn't been home for two years, the only time I had seen him was on the TV or in the papers or when I was doing publicity and I really wanted to see him.

Everyone had to go to bed at 9 p.m. so at ten to, a nurse came along and said, "Everyone in bed!" I explained I had permission to stay up but she refused to believe me and made such a fuss that she talked throughout the whole news and I couldn't hear a word my dad said once again.

I was so determined to hear him that I went to the matron and asked if I could stay up to watch the 10 p.m. news and she said I could. So I stayed up after everyone had gone to bed and there had been a hand-over to the night staff . When the night nurse spotted me she said, "It's bed time," and I told her I had been given permission to stay up.

"No, no, you're going to bed," she said. "No, I'm not going to bed, I've been told I could stay up." She said, "No," turned the TV off and said, "You ARE going to bed!" Just then she got called away and had to leave me so I hid under a chair and turned the TV back on very quietly. She looked in but couldn't see anyone so she left it on.

Ten o'clock came round and my dad was on the news once again but just as he was coming on, the night nurse came back in and spotted me. She shouted, "I told you to go to bed!" and I pleaded, "I've been told I could stay up," and then she tried to pick me up.

In order to pick me up in those days people relied on me to cinch my arms so they had something to grab. It was like lifting a sack of potatoes – if you don't hold it right round the middle it just slides out of your hands and I had a trick of lifting my hands up so people couldn't get a grip on me.

I did that when she tried to lift me and I slipped right out of her hands so she picked me up by the feet and, dangling me, wriggling with my full weight hanging from my feet, carried me to the ward and dumped me in bed.

I screamed all the way and was still screaming as she pulled the covers over me. I was in absolute agony. It was really, really painful. She said, "If you don't shut up, I'll give you something to cry about!" Matron came along doing a ward round, asked why I was crying and told the nurse she had given me permission to stay up for the news.

She asked me what was wrong and I sobbed, "My feet, my feet hurt." She pulled the covers back and my feet had swollen to twice their normal size. She asked the nurse, "How did you pick her up?" and she said, "I tried to pick her up round the waist but she lifted her arms up so I picked her up by her feet."

Matron made a cradle to keep the blankets off me and called the duty doctor. I was in so much pain that when the doctor put his little finger on my foot I screamed the place down again. They took me to x-ray which showed the nurse had crushed bones in both my feet.

She was sacked and I was in plaster from my feet all the way up to my waist for about a month. My feet were never the same after that and I never got to see the interview with my dad about the compensation.

The Thalidomide Children's Trust was set up in August, 1973 and the following year Harold Wilson's government paid a further £5 million into it to meet its tax liabilities. Awards were made according to a points system relating to the scale of disability. Mine was kept in trust until I was 21 when I asked them to keep hold of it until I was 25 and I've still got it except for what I have spent on education for my two children.

I have always been enormously proud of my dad and I think he did a brilliant job not just for me but for all the thalidomide children. It's because of his determination and cleverness at working out what we would need to live comfortably for the rest of our lives, taking inflation into account, that we have been able to live well and provide for our children.

But good things often come at a price and at the time Dad's campaign put enormous strain on him and my mother and caused me a huge amount of trouble and heartache through losing my friends and, worst of all, not being allowed to go home at all for two whole years. When Distillers finally settled, he was a hero to all those who had bad-mouthed him before but I think our family paid a big price for that compensation and I'll never get that back.

I read my dad's book as soon as it came out and found

that it only had a page and a half on me although it did include a lovely bit at the end in which he said I was just like any other child with all my ambitions for what I wanted to do in life. My reaction was, well, he doesn't really know me.

I didn't feel angry, I just felt I wanted to get to know him properly and for him to know me. I wanted to show him who I was, and for him to know that I wasn't the cabbage that it was feared I would be, that I did have a brain and I used it as much as I was capable of. I wanted him to know that I wasn't the kind of person to sit back and take bad treatment, that I had inherited his traits of being argumentative and stubborn. I wanted him to see himself in me but at the same time I didn't know how to show it because I hadn't got a close enough relationship with him.

While all the razzamatazz of the campaign was going on, however, I did, true to my nature, find another source of comfort besides my animals and that was in my friendship with a volunteer helper called Jill Fielding. She used to come to Chailey on Tuesdays and Thursdays to help out, make the beds, help dress the children, wash their hair and play with them.

She had short white hair and blue eyes and was a truly gentle, motherly person. I had a special link with her because she loved animals and I was besotted with them. We both had the same attitude to animals which involved a lot of respect, going far beyond love.

Volunteer helpers like her came and went and I usually didn't make much of a connection with them but with her it was different. I needed help putting my legs on and, as I was always very chatty, we got talking. I asked her where she lived and she said it was just under Ditchling Beacon which is a beautiful viewpoint on the South Downs.

She told me she had a house with a big pond. At the time I had a couple of great crested newts which I had kept from tadpoles but they were not eating well and needed to be released so she said she would put them in her pond. She kept koi carp in the pond and she brought me a copy of Aquarium Magazine and helped me look after my goldfish, then she brought me copies of Horse and Hound and dog magazines.

For the second Christmas that I was not allowed home, in 1972, Jill asked me if I would like to spend it at her house. We drove there in her yellow MG sports car with my wheelchair in the back, went right over Ditchling Beacon, down a tiny lane, through a farm gate and there was a huge pond, the same size as my garden now, on the right and a big paddock on the left. The driveway carried on to end in a set of garages and an enormous house on the right. I was not expecting anything like it and was absolutely stunned.

In the kitchen I met her dogs; she had loads of them including a German Shepherd, and a Dachshund, plus a couple of cats and a lamb which was called Brandy because it had been out in the snow and got very cold and the mother had died so she had brought it in and fed it brandy. Then we went into the front room and she had a big open fire. I had never been in a house with a fire like that, except my parents', it was so warm and she had tangerines on the table.

Jill was married to a racehorse trainer and I later found out they were going through marital discord and she had volunteered at Chailey to get herself out of the house. She had a son and a daughter, aged about 21 and 18, the elder of whom was at university, and she treated me just like one of the family. I wasn't used to being in a family situation other than my own and at first I felt awkward, like I was intruding, but she made a really special effort to make me feel at home. That night I was carried upstairs and put in a big old bed with a really thick mattress and lots of blankets in a bedroom which had a nightlight in a mushroom shape.

In the morning I woke up and, though she had only decided on the spur of the moment to take me for Christmas, she had done a stocking for me with fruits and nuts in the bottom and some chocolate and when I got downstairs I found my mum and dad had sent a present which had miraculously turned up under her tree.

Jill had got me a present as well and we had a really good Christmas. It was the first of many visits of which I have very fond memories. I loved watching her doing the cooking; I remember we always had corn on the cob with loads of butter and salt and bread. I used to go to the paddock and watch the stables staff train the racehorses on the lunge rein – I adored horses. On Saturday evening the family would gather in the living room and I would sit on the floor between them.

During those years I saw a lot more of Jill Fielding than of my own family but the visits came to an end when she and her husband split up and she had to work and I lost touch with her altogether after I left Chailey.

A few years later when I was married and my daughter, Emma, was a baby, I decided to take my husband John on a day trip to see the place where I had been brought up. While we were looking round Chailey it suddenly occurred to me to go and see if Jill Fielding was still living in her lovely house.

I remembered what it looked like but I couldn't recall exactly where it was. We drove around until I finally recognised it but the people living there told us she had moved after she got divorced. The search seemed hopeless but I was determined to find her. I had had this feeling for months that I needed to see her.

I suddenly remembered that she had told me she had met another man who was a keen gardener and that they had a big greenhouse. By then we had spent about an hour going around her village of Hassocks, Sussex, which is a one-street place with a lot of little lanes going off it and John, who didn't have a lot of patience, was kicking up a fuss saying, "Oh come on, let's go. We've been here for hours."

I persuaded him to try going down one more lane and there was a large greenhouse. I said, "This is it, I'm sure it is." John said, "No, it can't be," but he agreed to get out and knock on the door. A man answered and John said, "I'm sorry, but is there somebody here called Jill Fielding, or used to be?" and when the man said there was, he said, "Well, I've got Louise Mason here, as she used to be."

I was thrilled to have found her but very sad as well as her new husband told us she was suffering from cancer of the spine. He said that she was really bad, there was no cure and that she was upstairs basically waiting to die. John carried me upstairs and I spent an hour or two with her. She was amazed to see me like that, out of the blue. She died a month later but I was so glad I'd followed my instincts and found her again before it was too late.

Chapter Five
Teenage Years

I HAVE ALWAYS BEEN very mischievous, I love playing practical jokes, and as I grew bigger and stronger physically and mentally I often got into trouble at Chailey. I remember one spring a troupe of army cadets rented the sports hall to sleep in for the night while they were on manoeuvres and I and three or four other girls decided to play a really rotten trick on them.

They had put up their camp beds in rows in the hall and had gone out on the common. We took the balls of wool we used for crocheting, which was all the rage at the time, and tied one end to one bed then looped the wool round the top ends of the other beds so they were all linked together.

The wool was grey and so was the floor so at night the wool could hardly be seen. We tied the end of the wool to the fire door which we knew was the way they would come in as the other door was padlocked. The idea was that when they opened the fire door all the beds we had looped together would be turned upside down and their kit would fly all over the place.

We had also made itching powder by collecting red berries, crushing them and drying them out and we sprinkled this in their sleeping bags. Oh, we were really, really naughty. The next day the whole school was summoned to the dining hall and the chaplain announced sternly, "Somebody has done something to the soldiers in the sports hall and I want the guilty parties to come forward."

One of the boys put his hand up and asked what had gone

wrong and the chaplain said, "Somebody has done a practical joke and when one of the soldiers opened the fire door all of a sudden the beds tipped over and we found this," and he presented the wool. The other girls and I looked at each other but we managed to keep our faces straight. The army never came back.

That same year we found a poor little fox curled up shivering and absolutely petrified in our film room where the projector and screen were kept. The previous year my sister, Claire, had gone foxhunting and had come home covered in blood as she had been "blooded" for the first time. She loved it but, being besotted by animals of all kinds as I was, I was dead against it.

The fox hunt often used to ride across the common and around Chailey but we were determined not to let the hounds or the huntmaster get to our little fox. We stood outside and refused to let them pass and in the end they had to go away empty-handed.

I was growing into a very determined young lady and, looking back, I can see how I sometimes came over as aggressive. But in my view the care staff treated us aggressively in the sense that if we didn't comply with the rules we were quite harshly punished.

The punishments ranged from going to bed with no tea to polishing everybody's shoes in the dormitory. There were 36 people, that's 72 shoes, and they weren't just polished like you do now with cream in a tube, I'm talking about proper spit and polish. You would be there from 6 p.m. to 9 p.m. polishing 72 shoes. You just had to pray there had not been any football that day.

At 11 I had moved to the senior section of Chailey, called St George's, and started secondary school where our equipment was becoming more sophisticated. We were taught to use a POSSUM, which was basically a typewriter with a hand control moulded to your needs. Each letter had a combination of two micro switches you had to press. For instance, A was 22, B was 35, C was 33, D was 43, E was 21, and so on. A metal bar came up from the typewriter and on top of this was a white box on which the micro switches were mounted. I got up to 70 words per minute; in fact I got too fast for the box to recognise what I was typing.

Generally speaking, however, the most anyone achieved at 16 was five CSEs, which was the exam for those judged not clever enough to take GCEs. This was because our lessons were so disrupted by always being taken out of school for physiotherapy or to see the occupational therapist or for a health check or for any old doctor who happened to be visiting to have a go at pulling at our arms and legs.

I was beginning to protest against things I didn't like and top of the list of things I hated was the fact I had no rights over my own body: they could just call me over and do whatever they wanted to me. Worst of all was the annual health check-up that I used to call the MOT test, part of which involved injecting me with a dye. As a Thalidomider with no major limbs, I have no main veins so they wanted to see how well my blood was circulating. They also measured my limbs and took photographs from every angle.

When I started maturing and my breasts were developing I fiercely objected to having to strip naked for this examination. In addition there was the indignity involved in injecting me with the dye. The only place they could do this was in my feet but as my feet got tougher they found it increasingly difficult to locate a vein to put the needle in. They tried sitting me for half an hour in a warm bucket of water but still no veins came up in my feet though one did come up in my chest.

One of the doctors, called Dr Schneider, who was not a friendly man and tended to treat you like a laboratory animal, arrived with a nurse and Miss Derby, the radiographer, who was very nice and had a little white dog I liked.

The doctor laid me on the couch and said, "We are going to inject into her bust." And then he added, "Obviously, she is not going to have any children," at which I just screamed. I wanted to have children and I certainly didn't want an injection in my chest because those IVPs hurt, I hated them.

I couldn't bear the embarrassment of having to sit there naked when I was maturing, then to be told I was going to be injected with this dye into my breast but it didn't matter because I was never going to have children. I screamed and squealed and made a real fuss until Miss Derby eventually intervened and stopped it. I was the last or nearly the last to have the IVP because they decided after that it was too much of a hassle and too stressful for us to go through with it. But they still took photos of us every year in vest and pants.

As well as becoming more rebellious, I was also becoming more thoughtful about my situation in other ways, a process that began when I went on a trip to Lourdes in 1973. Coincidentally, it was at Lourdes that I met my first husband, John, although "met" is not exactly the right word. "Almost killed" would be nearer the mark, as I will explain.

Lourdes is a small town in the foothills of the French Pyrenees where apparitions of Our Lady appeared to a young girl called Bernadette Soubirous in 1858. It now plays host to around five million pilgrims and tourists every year who come from all over the world. Many of them are very sick and come hoping St Bernadette will intercede for them and perform a miracle cure.

A group was going from the local Catholic church, organised by a Dr Stroud. He invited people from Chailey to join it and, as my mum had a Catholic background, even though I was being bought up as Church of England at Chailey, I was allowed to go. I was fairly well steeped in religion anyway because I had to go to church every Tuesday, Thursday and Sunday and perform in a nativity play every year. Also there was a warden at St George's called Miss Fields who used to read us chapters from the Bible. She read the chapters suited to the season and as we got older we could pick the chapters we wanted. So I knew the Bible inside out, and I was in the choir.

Lourdes was a very big experience for me. I had to go to London then get a train to Portsmouth, take the ferry – I was seasick, of course – then another train. At the hotel they put me in a room with a girl from Chailey, called Sharon Birch, and another young girl from somewhere else whose name I never knew.

Sharon had brittle bones and arthritis. She was a year older than me and a prefect and she was really nice; I looked up to her but they made us share a double bed, which I hated. The other girl was in a single bed at the bottom of the double.

We had been there two or three days when I remember waking up in the middle of the night and seeing the figure of Our Lady, dressed in a white nun's habit, standing in our room. She had a glow all around her and she was bending down over the girl at the end of our bed. As I stared at her she said softly, "Close your eyes now, I'm taking this girl with me." I said, "OK," and went back to sleep.

The next day I got up feeling different. I don't know how, just different. We had to go down to prayers before breakfast then more prayers before we went out. As Sharon and I were dressing, the other girl didn't move. I knew she was very ill and that coming to Lourdes had been her last hope but we didn't know her so didn't like to disturb her.

On our way to prayers I told someone the other girl hadn't stirred. They went and saw her then there was a great big fuss all over the hotel. Dr Stroud raced to her room, followed by some nuns while we were packed off to the sacred Grotto.

All day I felt really mellow and different. After things calmed down, I said to Dr Stroud, "Bernadette took her, didn't she?" He said, "What do you mean?" I said, "I don't mean Bernadette, I mean that lady," pointing to the picture of Our Lady. He demanded to know what I was talking about and I told him what I had seen. It turned out the girl had died just at the time I had seen Our Lady.

After we had been there four or five days I knew the area well and liked looking around by myself in my wheelchair which I propelled along with a pair of crutches. Surrounded by all these sick people, I felt more full of energy than ever and I liked going fast.

The hotel was on a hill and one day I was coming down it so fast I couldn't stop myself. As I hurtled along shouting, "Move out of the way!" I saw a lady with a blond-haired boy who both leaped off the pavement just in the nick of time.

I thought no more of it until years later when John and I

were going through each other's photographs from the years before we met. He brought out one, saying, "That's when we were at Lourdes." I asked him what year he went and he said, "It was 1973, in April. And I was having a really good time until some stupid girl came thundering down the hill in her wheelchair and nearly ran me over. My mum then attached me firmly to her side for the whole of the rest of the trip."

At the end of the week there was the pilgrimage procession when all the groups come out and walk together to the chapel in the underground grotto. During one of Our Lady's apparitions to St Bernadette, she asked that people come in procession to the grotto where there is a spring whose water is said to have healing powers. The chapel is huge, in the shape of an enormous circle with a pulpit in the middle.

Everyone who was in Lourdes that week gathered there and sang a few songs. As we left we were each given a plastic cup with a candle on the top and the words of a hymn written on the side which everyone sang as they walked around the town. Thousands and thousands joined in a great procession, all with their candles, all singing the same. It was overwhelming. I felt very sad the next day to be packing my bags as it had been a truly eye-opening and spiritual experience.

Seeing so many people who were suffering in different ways at Lourdes, and reading about my own birth in my father's book, got me thinking about disability and led me on to read a lot more. I researched the history of disability right back to biblical times, interested in why disabled people were treated so differently. I wondered why lepers were put in leper colonies. When Jesus was curing the lame, what was lame? Where and how did they live?

I realised that disability had not really been studied as a subject: it was a part of history that had been kept hidden. And disabled people are still treated very differently in different parts of the world. You see the pictures of children in Romanian orphanages which is how things were in this country in the past, whereas what we do now is generally where America was 20 or 30 years ago.

All this research helped me understand how society's

attitudes impacted on me. In the 70s disabled people were just beginning to come out of institutions and live in the community, mixing with able-bodied people. What I felt was disabled but healthy. I didn't need or want to be with sick people. I wasn't sick, like so many were at Lourdes, I just happened to be without arms and legs.

I didn't need medical help, I needed to get muddy and go climbing and get into mischief. Chailey portrayed us Thalidomiders as being the worst affected people there because we had no legs and arms, but going to Lourdes made me realize we were not the worst because we were not ill. There were people suffering and dying, we were living.

As time went by, and society as a whole started becoming more open to disabled people, I started to go out more, which meant coming to terms with how I looked. At first I wasn't really aware of looking different because in Chailey everyone was different. In fact, the situation gave me a bit of an attitude to anyone who looked normal as being someone who could only be there for my benefit. Provided they were over 16, walking around and apparently mentally normal, as far as I was concerned, they were there to help me. But when we ventured out, we had to get used to the stares.

In the early 70s I started going to a Saturday morning movie club which was one of those old riotous affairs of a cinema full of boisterous kids, a bunch of cartoons, a break for an icecream, then the main film. Then on Thursday nights we started going to a youth club in Haywards Heath which had a disco.

At first I wore my artificial legs when I went there but because there were able-bodied teenagers there as well, I was very wary of being knocked over.

I thought wearing my legs might increase my chances of getting dances but after going to the disco three or four times I realised it wasn't making any difference whether I was walking or in a wheelchair so I didn't bother with the legs any more. In a wheelchair you could really mess around; if a boy wanted a slow dance he could get on his knees by the chair though that never happened to me. It was really good fun and it got the community involved. They knew Chailey was there, somewhere up the hill, but this was proper integration.

A little bit later they started letting us go to Burgess Hill market on Saturday mornings which consisted of about ten shops including a Tesco and a pet shop. I would go straight to the pet shop to look at the goldfish, play with the hamsters and get provisions for my animals, then I'd spend my pocket money on enough crisps, peanuts and chocolate for the week.

Most of the time we went out as a group and people didn't take a lot of notice but when I was on my own I found people's attitude was a bit wary. But we had been taught to be determined and independent and if somebody looked at you, it was fine.

Kids are wonderful, they don't judge you. They would stare but I always found that if you smiled at a child, he or she would smile back. Occasionally one would ask: "Why haven't you got any arms or legs?" and I would always explain that it was because my mum took a bad pill.

When I was on holiday as an older teenager at a hotel the Thalidomide Trust owns in Jersey, I liked going for a walk on my own on the beach and I learned that people were either scared of me or concerned. They often asked where my carer was and if I needed them to ring somebody to come and get me. I learned to be polite and to smile but to be determined and say: "No, I'm on my own and I'm fine, thank you."

Some people were not so pleasant, perhaps unintentionally. One time I was coming out of Tesco in Burgess Hill having bought a raw jelly which I absolutely loved at that time, when an adult came up to me and said straight out, "Why are you like how you are?" I said, "I've just beamed down from Mars and if you're not careful, I'll turn you purple," and he ran, he really ran! I felt guilty that I could be so horrible to somebody who just asked a question.

There were some children at Chailey who suffered cruel treatment not from strangers but from their own families. I knew of one girl who was sexually abused by her father for five years. I believe the staff knew about it but did nothing.

Another boy used to go home for the holidays and I

remember that in the very hot summer of 1976 he came back early, right in the middle of the holidays. No one came back early to Chailey unless something had gone wrong but when I saw his dad's car drive up, I was excited to see him. We were all wearing tops and shorts and I toddled up to him and gave him a big hug. He had a shirt on and I said, "It's so hot, take your shirt off." He was sweating buckets but he wouldn't take his shirt off no matter how much I teased. In the end I pulled his shirt up and saw these marks on his back so I went up to a male staff nurse and he asked, "What's wrong? You seem troubled." I said, "If I tell you something, will you not say where it came from?" He promised so I told him about my worries about my friend coming back early, refusing to take his shirt off and the marks I saw on his back.

The staff nurse called the boy over and called the doctor who found he had whip marks all down his back, about three or four days old. I asked him what happened and he said "Nothing," but I kept on and eventually he said, "If you really want to know, my dad taught me how to fall over on my artificial legs. He pushed me over so I learned how to fall this way and that way."

At the beginning of the following term I noticed that whenever he wore his artificial legs, he would walk alongside a wall so that if he fell the wall would support him. And if he was going to cross a room he would first make sure there was no one else around who could possibly knock him over. The school noticed his strange behaviour too and I began to suspect he hadn't told me the full story. So after a while I asked him what had actually happened in the summer holidays. He said, "If I was walking on my artificial legs my dad would come past and push me. But he said that if I fell over, I would get the strap."

I suppose his dad wanted to teach him how to fall over so that he would do less damage to himself if he did fall, or not to fall over at all. His method of doing this was that, whenever my friend fell, he whipped him with a belt. My friend had been home for four weeks and had obviously fallen over – and been pushed – a lot. Three or four months later he gave up his legs for good saying he couldn't handle them any more. Chailey didn't do anything about his dad's whippings, but he was the only kid they allowed to give up wearing artificial legs.

Whatever my parents were like, I was very proud of them, especially my dad for winning the fight for proper compensation, and I didn't suffer the abuse, either physical or psychological, that a lot of the other Thalidomiders did. Yet they didn't treat me the same as my siblings.

I remember my 13th birthday really well because I had a recurrence of a bout of typhoid which I had first caught on a holiday in Majorca the year before. I was put into isolation and a couple of days before my birthday I was delirious. On the day itself I was beginning to recover and my Auntie Hilary, who always bought me some nice perfume, came down for my birthday.

I thought it was an important age, my 13th birthday. My sister, Claire's birthday had been in October and she had got a horse, Lindsey's had been in March and she had got riding lessons and David's had been on June 21 and he had got a big stereo system. So I was all hopeful of getting something really special.

A large parcel had been delivered the day I was taken to hospital and when Auntie Hilary came I opened her present of Charlie perfume which I still like the smell of. Then I excitedly tore open this really big parcel from my mum and dad and it was a frigging suitcase. I thought there was bound to be something fantastic inside it. Yeah – paper. I felt incredibly disappointed.

As they got older, my brother and sisters got given cars, they got horses, they got houses. I sometimes thought, oh if only I had been like them, I would have got that. They had it all on a plate but things didn't come so easy to me. I never asked my mum and dad for anything. I gave up when I kept asking to go home and nothing happened. I think my 13th birthday was the last time I asked to come home; and I got a suitcase.

But everything comes at a price, I reckon, and the price for getting the things my siblings have been given was having to live with my dad who is a bit of a control freak and likes to be the patriarch of the family. After my sister was given a car she swore at my dad and he took the car back. When I bought my house with my compensation, I could have sworn at my dad as much as I liked (although I never did) and he could never have taken it back.

In my early teens boy-girl relationships followed the usual pattern of experimental fumblings. I had grown friendly with Grahame Tindale again after all the publicity over the compensation battle had finished. We would play tricks on each other, like making apple pie beds, but we would also sit and talk, telling each other things we wouldn't tell anyone else. At the same time we were always falling out over something or another – just like a normal brother and sister, I suppose.

When I was 12 or 13 a lot of the other kids used to call us boyfriend and girlfriend. There was a room we used to call the drying room because it was full of heating pipes and they would put the clothes to dry there. One day some horrible kid shut us in there shouting that we should have some private time together to see what sex was like.

We couldn't do that. I'd been in the same bath with him, slept in the same cot with him. He was more like my brother than my own brother. We were both on the floor without our wheelchairs and we couldn't reach the lock so with the heat from the pipes we began to dehydrate quite quickly. It felt like we were in there for hours though it was probably only ten minutes before one of the wardens came by and opened the door and we fell out, panting.

There was quite a lot of sexual experimentation going on at Chailey though I didn't know too much about it at 13 until something really horrible happened. I started going out with a particular boy of the same age who had something wrong with his legs but had normal arms. One day he asked me to go to his room to listen to some music. I went to everyone's room so I didn't think twice about going.

He said, "Come and sit on the edge of the bed." So we sat side by side and the next thing I knew he was on top of me and started raping me. He was built like a gorilla, top heavy and very strong in his arms and I had no chance of getting away from him.

I was crying and obviously distressed and in the middle of all this, one of the care staff walked in, saw what was going on, just said, "Oh", and shut the door. I was sobbing, shocked and bleeding when the boy finally let me go. I got off the bed and climbed into my wheelchair feeling numb and alienated and dirty.

I immediately went up to one of the care staff and said I wanted to go to the loo, could someone help me, which they did. I was very disorientated, devastated and in a lot of pain. As the nurse took my knickers down she said, "There's blood," and I said, "I know, I've been raped." She said, "Oh no, it's just your periods starting. You are the right age." I said, "No, it's not. You can ask one of the care staff who walked in." She said, "Yes, it is."

She dismissed it. She didn't believe me. No matter how much I argued and told her what had really happened no one would accept what I said. They just totally ignored it, as if it was something that could not possibly happen, or shrugged and said that in any event I would start my periods the next month. In fact I didn't start for six months.

No one was listening to me so I went to the dispensary because I was very sore from blisters on the back of my legs, which they used to put methylated spirits on. They saw how distressed I was and sent me to the doctor. After he examined me, he turned to the nurses and said, "Did you know she is not intact?" and they said, "Oh well, it doesn't matter."

Nothing happened to the boy. The man who walked in on us said he didn't see anything. Chailey was going through a very difficult stage, like all society was, as it was slowly being acknowledged that disabled people had sexual feelings just like anyone else. It was still a topic people were not comfortable talking about. Sex and disabled didn't go together.

Chailey said it couldn't happen, so it hadn't happened. I was angry but by that time I had become a master at shutting things away. Remembering, definitely remembering, but pushing the emotion so far down that nobody could get to it.

Slowly through my teens I learned how to cope with society at large; how to be friendly with people but also to educate them that just because externally you are a disabled person outside doesn't mean you are disabled on the inside.

I've found that you should treat people the way you want to be treated. You need to be outgoing, to talk to people, break the ice yourself and be friendly and open as much as you can. But you also have to be determined so they don't walk over you. I always do my best to make it clear that I am not going to be treated any differently just because I'm in a wheelchair.

Hopefully, if you approach people this way, they will see beyond the skin which is just an outer layer. I've tried to teach my kids it doesn't matter what you look like from the outside, the colour of your skin or your nationality. You should try and see beyond all that because it's what's inside that counts and that's what people should look for.

Chapter Six
Leaving Chailey

In my last term at Chailey I got the most prestigious award the school bestowed. Called the Seymour Overmore prize, it was a lifetime achievement award in recognition not just of academic success but of how you had coped with all the problems posed by your disability. So it was chiefly about your attitude, your initiative, your spirit and was highly regarded by all my contemporaries.

I had responded to the competitive spirit fostered at Chailey and had been the first to learn to do many things for myself. Notably, I had been the first four-limbs deficient Thalidomider to be able to put my own artificial legs on and take them off. I had learned two years previously and it meant I didn't have to wait for care staff to do it. They just needed to stand me up on my legs between strapping one person in and another and I could do the rest myself and always be on time for school. Coming back from school it was even better because while everyone else had to wait to have their legs taken off, which was a pain when you had been in them since 7.30 a.m., I could come straight in at 4.30 p.m., whip them off and I was away.

I was not told that I was going to get the Seymour Overmore award until the morning of the annual prize-giving when the staff started treating me like royalty. I knew my parents would have been invited – parents didn't come to every prize-giving but were especially invited if you had won this top prize. Usually the parents made a lovely great fuss of the winner and proudly accompanied him or her to have a cup of tea with the headmaster before the ceremony.

When I was told I was getting it, I felt extremely chuffed and was looking forward to the look of pride in my parents' eyes as they watched me walk through the packed hall to the stage to receive it. I dressed excitedly in my most fashionable clothes – long boots on my artificial legs, a skirt that met the top of the boots and a check shirt, and went down to the school entrance to look out for them.

Then my grandma, Dad's mum, turned up, alone. Much as I loved her, I wanted my mum and dad to be there. I didn't want anyone else. But they didn't come because my grandma said my father was busy and she was standing in for them. I felt gutted, cheated. I couldn't believe they wouldn't be there to see my proudest moment out of 16 years at Chailey, getting public recognition for all I had struggled to achieve. I was completely devastated.

There was nothing I could do except swallow my terrible disappointment and resolve not to let it spoil my enjoyment of getting the award. My grandma came with me to the headmaster's office and we sat down for our cup of tea. Then we went into the prize-giving and when it came to the Seymour Overmore award, it was a bit like the Oscars. No one else knew who had won it because you were not allowed to tell anyone and they didn't announce the name straight away. Instead they described you and what you had done.

So the headmaster started talking about how I'd turned up at Chailey at five weeks old. He described all the things I'd learned to do, including being the first to put my own legs on, and so on, then he announced my name and I walked up to collect the award as everyone applauded. Later on my name was added to the big plaque which still hangs in Chailey's assembly hall.

That was a big, big day for me. After the ceremony my grandma gave me a box of chocolates that was supposed to be from my parents. I never asked them why they didn't come. By that time I had been so disappointed so many times that I didn't bother to ask.

I was now 17 and my time at Chailey was coming to an end. Decisions had to be made about how I was to manage the rest of my life. At the beginning of that summer term the headmaster had done my assessment and asked my parents to come down any time that suited them to discuss it.

One morning I was told my parents were coming. I felt pleased and excited, eager to talk over my plans to go to college to improve my education so I could get a reasonable job to support myself in the independent life which I was determined to have.

When I walked into the head's office, my parents were already there and I heard them talking about sending me to a home for disabled adults called John Grooms. This was the first I had heard of this plan and it came like a blow to the stomach. It was the very last place I wanted to go. I knew there was absolutely no way I could live in a home. I hated being confined. You had a bedroom and that was it: everything you have is in that room. I could not bear the thought and was very shocked and disappointed.

The head, who knew me very well, saw how upset I was and asked my parents to wait outside. Then he asked me what was wrong and I wailed, "I don't want to go into a home, I want to improve my education. I know I'm not the brightest spark on the street but I'm not the stupidest. And I know I can do something useful with my life."

Next he got my parents in and sent me out. After a while his secretary came out to ask if I was all right and I sobbed in turn to her: "My parents want to send me to a home!" I was really overcome.

After a while my parents came out and said, "We've got to go now," so I walked them to the car. I'd been expecting them to take me out to lunch as deciding on the future course of your life was a pretty special occasion, it seemed to me, but they handed over a great big box of fancy chocolates and said goodbye.

I had to go back to see the head after lunch. I walked in even more adamant that I was not going to go into a home and before he had a chance to say anything I announced, "I'm not going." He told me he had convinced my parents I shouldn't go to John Grooms, which was a big relief, so then we started talking over the other options. At that time the suitable residential places in the South-west of England were St Lewis's College in Exeter, Devon, and the National Star Centre in Cheltenham, Gloucestershire.

I went to look round St Lewis's and everything seemed fine. But after I had decided on it, they said they couldn't take someone who was four-limbs deficient because they had never done it. It was infuriating because the place was for the disabled and I could manage as well as anybody else in my wheelchair. So Chailey helped me fight against it, accusing the college of discrimination. They finally caved in but by then I felt awkward about going because I'd be notorious for causing such a stink so I decided to go to the Star Centre at Cheltenham instead.

I left Chailey officially in July, 1979. I went on holiday for two weeks to the Thalidomide Trust hotel in Jersey and then straight on to another Thalidomide Trust holiday in Gran Canaria. But I had nowhere to go for the last two weeks of the summer holiday so I returned to Chailey until I could start at the Star Centre. It was not an option to go to my parents'. They had told me that if I was old enough and independent enough not to go to a home, then I was independent enough to sort myself out.

I'm sure they were doing what they thought was in my best interests. I'd lived in an institution my whole life where I had always had someone on hand to help me and they must have been asking themselves how I was I going to cope on my own. They were wondering what would happen in two years when the course at the Star Centre finished, but I was young and didn't think much further ahead than the next week.

The biggest wrench for me leaving Chailey was having to abandon my pets. Until that summer I had two terrapins, Tom and Tabitha. Tabitha had died when I was away on holiday because you are supposed to put olive oil on their shells and turn on the heat lamp. No one had done it, nor had they fed them, so Tabitha had expired and Tom had eaten her.

Jill Fielding took Tom while Chailey kept my 33 goldfish and Bungo, my rabbit. He was beautiful, black and tan, and lived in a specially adapted hutch I had bought for him with a door set high up so I could get him out. I later found out that someone had left his cage open and he'd escaped and was killed by a fox. They found a clump of his black and tan fur left behind on the common.

When I arrived at the Star Centre I only knew one person, Grahame Tindale, who had been there for a year already. He had got a girlfriend and was making himself a life so I didn't have a lot of contact with him but I soon settled down and made other friends.

When the first half-term holiday came around in October, Grahame asked me what I was going to do as the Centre would be closed. It was a week with a weekend at either end, so I had to find somewhere to go for ten days. I said didn't know, I hadn't thought about it. I rang my mum and dad and asked if I could come home for a week and they said no, so I was stuck. The only life I had known was Chailey but once you had left, that was it. It wasn't your home any more.

I spoke to the Thalidomide Trust who asked me what I wanted to do. I said I wanted to go to London; I suppose secretly I was hoping my parents would come and get me, or at least meet me. The Trust told me to book into a hotel and they would pay the bill but, being the independent type, I told them I thought I had enough money to pay up front and they could replace it by paying money into my Post Office account.

Then I rang the Bloomsbury Hotel and they told me it would cost about £20 a night which I thought was for bed and breakfast and an evening meal. I felt pretty pleased with myself and went round boasting that I was off to London for ten days.

So when the Centre closed for the break, I got on a National Express coach in Cheltenham, alighted at the coach station in Victoria in London and pushed myself from Victoria to the Bloomsbury Hotel, propelling my wheelchair along with my crutches with my rucksack hanging from the back. I booked myself in feeling really posh and smart and thought, yeah, great. Here I am!

A porter took my stuff upstairs and set the room up so I could manage. I sat there in this room with the big TV on and decided to make a plan. I would spend Saturday and Sunday getting used to the facilities in the hotel and exploring the immediate area. On Monday I was going to visit the Tate Gallery, Tuesday the Natural History Museum, Wednesday the National Gallery, Thursday the Victoria and Albert Museum and Friday the British Library. So at the weekend I went pottering around, got myself a drink and a snack and went back for dinner and an evening of TV in my room.

I had paid the hotel on arrival for Friday, Saturday and Sunday and when Monday came I had to pay for Monday night, Tuesday and Wednesday. So I went to the nearest Post Office and gave them my book. The system was then that, if they made a mistake, they had to send the book to Glasgow to get it rectified and you had to wait three days for it to come back.

Unfortunately, that's what happened. A mistake had been made which meant that all I could withdraw was £15. The book would have to be sent away and they said it should be back by the Wednesday. This left me in a bit of a fix, to put it mildly. I went back to hotel and told them what had happened and they said there was not a lot they could do.

They agreed to keep my stuff for me so I had an extra big breakfast, as much as I could stuff inside me, and off I toddled for an enjoyable day at the Tate Gallery. Come the night I had absolutely nowhere to go. I rang the Trust who told me to go back to the hotel and phone them from there but, being 17, I was too proud to turn up there again without the money to pay.

I was only round the corner from my dad's gallery but my pride refused to let me go there either and confess that I'd made a mess of my first trip away on my own. So I just trundled around London, sleeping for two nights on the streets in my wheelchair.

I budgeted the £15 so I could buy drinks and something to eat but I quickly ran out and I ended up starving. You use up an awful lot of calories pushing yourself around, especially when it turns chilly. By the third day my hunger pangs were truly painful. I lost a lot of weight.

I only had a bomber jacket but luckily it wasn't too cold. I hung around the streets nearest the hotel, hiding in doorways. I made sure I went into streets where no one else was and looked for a warm corner or a shop window. If anyone came I waited until they had taken four or five steps past me then I moved on. It was not so bad because in London you can stay in a gallery or somewhere until six then, by the time you have had something to eat – though I didn't have enough cash for a proper meal – and go to the loo and mess around in there for an hour or so, most of the evening has gone by.

People don't start getting suspicious about why a limbless person is out on the street in a wheelchair until 1 or 2 a.m. Then you have to hide away and be ready to move on until 6 a.m. when London starts coming to life again and you are no longer conspicuous.

At 9 a.m. on the Wednesday, I turned up at the Post Office but my book had not arrived. That was a very bad moment as I had been so looking forward to breakfast. I had to go back in the afternoon for the second post and luckily the book was there. I took out £50, returned to the hotel, paid for my room, had a shower and an enormous dinner, watched the movie and went to bed. Simple things like having a pillow to put my head on after two days were absolute bliss.

Looking back I realise it was not a sensible thing to do as I was incredibly vulnerable. But at the time I felt pleased with myself for having survived without asking anyone for help. It's an experience which has always stayed with me, giving me an understanding of homelessness and of hunger which I would not have had otherwise.

The next holidays were Christmas which was three weeks and I was still not welcome at home. After the shock of running out of money in London I decided not to risk anything like that again, but I had nowhere else to go. I rang the Thalidomide Trust who contacted Chailey and the upshot was I was invited to stay at Walsingham House in Hove on the Sussex coast which was a holiday home for long-term residents of Chailey, run by a retired member of staff.

That worked out OK but I had been allowed to stay there as a special favour which couldn't be repeated as I wasn't at Chailey any more. Back at the Star Centre it began to prey on my mind that the next half-term was looming in only six weeks. So I went to the principal who found a YWCA in Southampton which had just built a new section for the disabled and would take me.

On a cold, dark February day, I climbed aboard another National Express coach by myself, got to Southampton and took a taxi to the YWCA. I was shown my room, the TV room and little kitchenette and told the rules, including having to be in by a certain time, then I was on my own. The place stank of new paint and varnish and I felt very lost. I didn't know a soul, in a town I didn't know, and I was there for ten days.

I didn't sit about feeling sorry for myself, however. The next day I set off to explore the surrounding area and to go to the shops to get my supplies for the week. I found a Wimpy 100 metres down the road where I had my tea then pushed my way back – I was still pushing myself along with crutches.

On the way I noticed a red light across the road in front of my window which shone through the curtain all night. The next day I mentioned how hard it had been to sleep with this light shining into my room to one of the residents and she said, "Didn't you know that this is the middle of the red-light district?" I made sure I was home before dark after that.

Some days I pottered around the docks area, others round the shops in town but I was terribly lonely. I had no one to talk to. I spent a lot of time in my room feeling more and more desperate. One day I couldn't bear it and phoned the Thalidomide Trust social worker who came to see me and took me out but when she went away I was lonelier than ever.

I got up at 3 a.m. on the day I was to leave as I couldn't wait to get away. I stripped the bed, made sure all the pots and pans were clean and was out of the door by 6.30 a.m., heading for the bus stop where the coach was leaving from at 8 a.m. Back at the Star Centre I told the principal that though the YWCA had the right facilities for the disabled, the people had not been friendly and it had been a horrible experience because I was so dreadfully lonely.

Even so, when Easter came around I still had nowhere else to go so I was forced to return to Southampton. This time I took a friend, Jackie Fletcher, with me, but it wasn't much better. Though we had each other, we just felt lonely together.

The highlight of the holiday was when I decided to make toffee. I put the butter and sugar in a pan and asked Jackie to keep an eye on it while I did something else but she forgot and it all burned black. The whole place stank of burned toffee. It took a week to get it clean. I never went back there again. I couldn't stand it.

Meanwhile I was having a whale of a time at the Star Centre. I had a boyfriend, Darren (of whom more later), a Thalidomider whom I had met during the summer holidays, and I had made lots of other friends. I got on really well with the head and staff – I respected them, they respected me – and I had become the vice-president of the student union where we had a disco every Saturday evening.

I was beginning to spread my wings and felt my social skills and my independence growing stronger every day. On Thursday evenings a bunch of us ventured into the town centre by mini-bus where we congregated in a pub called the Brahms and Liszt. At about 10 p.m. I would go to the chip shop for a bit of refuelling, then go back to the pub for another drink or two and take a taxi back to the college. My life was definitely improving.

I started off doing business studies, art, maths and typing but unfortunately I got kicked out of art. We had two lady art teachers and they told me to draw anything I liked so I drew a man's posterior from the waist to the back of the knee. I did it in charcoal and pencil and I was extremely proud of it. It was really, really nice, as a bum goes.

I was so encouraged that I then did the front of a male. I spent ages on it, about two and a half weeks in lessons and breaks, but when I showed it to the teachers, it caused a bit of an uproar. I was accused of drawing offensive pictures and the head demanded to know who had been posing. It was Darren, but I had done it from memory, not had him posing at college, and I didn't think it was any of their business.

The problem really was that they still thought sex was something disabled people didn't do. They banned me from returning to art class which was a shame as I had loved it. But I felt absolutely no shame about what I had done. I told them it was nature. And secretly I was proud of doing something that so provoked them.

I switched to a drama class, not because I was interested in drama but I wanted to do English speaking because I knew that I didn't need arms and legs to use my voice. I worked up to the highest grade and took the exam in which you had to do a talk on a topic then answer questions. I achieved a distinction which pleased me greatly and the skills I learned have proved to be very useful. I also passed three exams in typing.

The rest of my holidays from the Star Centre were not nearly so grim, thank goodness. In the summer of 1980 I went to Walsingham House for three weeks but as a helper, not an ordinary resident. I had two weeks at the Trust hotel in Jersey and another week on a horse-riding holiday on Dartmoor at a place called Jollymead which had all the adaptations necessary for disabled people and really was jolly.

By then I had almost given up my artificial legs except for riding, which I loved. I got a National Express coach to Dartmoor where I was picked up but my legs were left behind on the coach. I had to spend the week mucking out the stables and cleaning the tack while everyone else went off riding. I ended up being put in a black bin liner, so I didn't get the mini dirty. It turned out the legs had gone to Edinburgh; they arrived the day before we left. I still had such fun that the next half-term I went back to Jollymead for a caving holiday.

As I neared the end of my two years at the Star Centre I had a discussion with the principal over what I would do next. My parents still wanted me to go into a home but I knew Grahame had used his compensation to buy his own home. I was still only 19 but I thought that if I got my own home I would be independent for ever.

Up until then I had only used little bits of my money

which was held in trust by the Thalidomide Trust. If I asked for anything I always felt like I was begging from them, even though it would come from my own allocation. The most I had asked them for was £199.99 for a black and white, portable TV, radio and cassette player for my room at college.

The Director of the Trust, Group Captain Gardiner, came to a review at the Star Centre – my parents stayed away – and we talked over where I wanted to live. I thought I would stay in Cheltenham as knew I could get around the town, it had a pace of life I could keep up with and I was already known and comfortable in some of the pubs and the chip shop.

It was agreed that social services should be involved so shortly afterwards I got a call from a social worker who asked when she could come and see me. I told her not Tuesday or Thursday as I helped in the student union on those days doing a chip-shop run on Tuesdays and a stock-take on Thursdays. So the next week she turned up, on the Thursday, when I was serving in the shop.

I was really cross. I said, "Why are you here today? You've come on a day when I specifically asked you not to come." I had just had enough of people in authority, of not having control over anything myself. But I realised I didn't have to comply with her agenda.

I took her to my room, shut the door and said, "The first thing you can do is get your diary out and make another appointment. I told you not to come on this day and you've come on this day when I've got other things to do." I gave her such a ribbing that she left in tears but I didn't care. I went back to the shop and got on with what I was doing.

That afternoon the principal summoned me to his office and introduced me to a great big Scottish bear of a man with black hair and a black beard. His name was Joe and he was the head of the town's Social Services department. He said he had heard I had given one of his social workers a hard time and that he took on difficult cases like me so he was taking me over.

There was no way I could live independently on my own, he told me, but there was a scheme which might be able to help me called Community Service Volunteers. They were usually gap year students, mostly 18- or 19-year-old girls, who worked for about four months at a time for pocket money. I could have one of those to live with me, monitored by a social worker.

I was thrilled when the Trust allocated me up to £30,000 to buy a house. It would be my very own place, I had never had any place I could call my own and I felt it was time. My only worry was that I would have another attack of the loneliness I'd endured in Southampton. I had spent my whole life with lots of people around me and having a whole house of my own would be very different. I just hoped the CSV would be enough of a companion.

I registered with a lot of estate agents who came to the Star Centre to pick me up and take me to places but nothing was suitable. Time was pressing and it was looking hopeless when the original social worker turned up again and took me to a place which had been converted for a disabled person and was available to rent.

I hated it on sight. The kitchen had been lowered so that the surfaces were more reachable from a wheelchair which made it look really odd. It was a place for the disabled and it looked like it. I wanted somewhere with good access where I could adapt things to suit me but which looked like a normal house in the first place.

I was just beginning to despair when I found the house, which I still live in. It was a spacious bungalow on a street within easy reach of Cheltenham town centre, set back off the road to give some privacy and with a drive big enough for a couple of cars. I liked it because it had character, though every room was either clad in pine or decorated in a dolly mixture of colours. Apart from the decorations, it was just what I wanted. As soon as I went in, it felt right.

It was a bit more than my budget and it needed rewiring and some adaptations such as having a ramp put in but once the head of the Trust, Group Captain Gardiner, had checked it over he said I could draw some money from the following year's allocation to cover the extra costs.

The work was going to take four months and I was in a dilemma about what I was going to do for all that time. I was still friendly with Grahame who was living with his girlfriend, Sharon, and he offered to let me stay in their back room. This was great at first as we talked and talked, just like old times. I had got an adapted car and was having driving lessons three times a week. Grahame came out with me for practice drives and we had a lot of fun.

In fact, we got on so well that Sharon started getting jealous. I tried to reassure her by saying that Grahame was like a brother to me because we had grown up together but she was not convinced and things began to get a bit heated.

It was something of a relief all round when the Trust agreed to pay for me to stay in a hotel for the last two weeks of this waiting period. And it was there that I began my new way of life with my first CSV helper, who was to become a lifelong friend and my maid of honour when I got married.

Nicky was 19, the same age as me, a gap-year student from Maidstone, Kent. She was bubbly, outgoing, pretty, intelligent and down to earth, except she didn't know how to boil an egg. She had never been away from home and I had never slept in a room with someone I didn't know, and we were chucked in the same hotel room for two weeks, together 24/7.

It was awkward at first but fortunately we got on from the start. When the two weeks came to an end, my very own house was ready and I began the life I had always yearned for – in a proper home I could call my own.

Chapter Seven
Love And Marriage

In SEPTEMBER 1981, I collected the keys to my three-bedroom bungalow, the first house I could truly call home, and arrived at the door at 9 a.m. with all I possessed – three suitcases of clothes and my little black and white portable TV/radio. That was it, I had no furniture, curtains, bed linen, crockery, cutlery or kitchen utensils but I did have something much more precious to me – a fabulous feeling of "Wow! This is mine!"

The Thalidomide Trust had allocated me £250 to get furniture and other essentials so my CSV carer, Nicky, and I breezed into town and had a fantastic shopping spree buying a double and a single bed, quilts and pillow sets, a second-hand settee and an armchair, a smoked glass-topped table and chairs, pots and pans, some plates, glasses, mugs and cutlery. I also bought myself a wall unit for storing my new stuff and a new small TV. It was brilliant.

When it had all been delivered we had to decide where it should go, and that's when the problems started. Nicky had quite different ideas to me and we had a row. We still hadn't known each other long and it all got a bit out of hand and she decided she wanted to go home.

This was not a good beginning to my brand new independent life so, feeling a bit panicked, I rang Joe, the head of social services who had pronounced me a difficult case and taken me on himself, and he came round and asked what the problem was. I said, "This is MY house. I'll have things where I want them." Joe told Nicky that she was only there for four months while it was my home for the foreseeable future and I could put things wherever I wanted to.

It might sound petty but to be able to do exactly what I liked, when I liked, was a completely novel experience for me. Initially, it went to my head and I did some pretty bizarre things. I had breakfast at dinner time, lunch at breakfast time and dinner whenever I felt like it, just because I could. I discovered the joys of Citizens' Band radio and decided most of the interesting people were on at night so I stayed in bed until 2 p.m. then got up and talked to my growing band of CB friends all afternoon and all night.

In the November I passed my driving test which opened up another whole new area of freedom. Unfortunately Nicky's time was up. During her time with me she had met Kelvin, who later became her husband, but she stayed around the Cheltenham area, not far from me. More CSV carers followed her. Then the following April, in 1982, I started at the Queen Elizabeth Training College in Leatherhead, Surrey, on a course to improve my office skills to give me a better chance of getting a job.

I stayed there during the week and came home at weekends, driving myself to and fro. I was still going out with Darren so some weekends I went to Birmingham to see him. At the college I began to get friendly with John Medus who was particularly kind and helpful to me. If I needed a push up the hill, he'd be the one to push me.

He was not tall, just 5ft 4ins, with blond hair and greenish blue eyes. He was registered blind because he suffered from severe nystigmus which made his eyes shoot backwards and forwards. The effect was like looking at life through a permanent torrential downpour. We got on fantastically well because he was great fun and adventurous; his attitude was: if we want to do something, we won't give up until we have found a way to do it, also he really made me laugh.

Most people went home from college at weekends but John only got a travel permit every other week so one weekend when he was going to be stuck in Leatherhead I invited him to come to Cheltenham. We talked a lot about everything under the sun, went to the pub together and had so many laughs.

He started coming to stay regularly at weekends, just as a friend, and happened to be here when I found out Darren had cheated on me, which broke my heart at the time. John comforted me and a bit later he asked me out and soon we became more than friends. We worked so well as a team; he was good at gardening, I was good at cooking. We had the same sense of humour, we were both game for anything and we both liked animals, particularly dogs. He couldn't drive, but I loved driving. I couldn't get out of the car by myself, so he helped me. He was my arms and legs and I was his sight. It was like we were two halves but when we were together, we made a whole. He was the man of my dreams.

Being with him gave me such a warm feeling. It was like someone had turned on the lights.

Not everyone had such a rosy attitude towards our relationship, however, particularly John's mother. His father was really nice; he didn't say a lot though when he did say something it was always worth listening to, but his mother didn't like me. I was not the girl she had dreamed of for a daughter-in-law and she didn't want her precious son getting serious about me.

The first time she saw me was at Queen Elizabeth College about a month after John and I had met when she and his dad came to take him home for half-term. He wanted to introduce me to them but I was nervous because I knew from experience what people's reactions were when they first saw me. They usually saw the outside shell, the Thalidomider in a wheelchair with no proper limbs, and couldn't see past that to the me inside.

We were outside when they arrived and, as they approached, I quickly pushed myself behind one of those decorative garden walls with holes in and hid. From there I overheard John saying to his mum: "I want you to meet Louise," and her replying: "Why are you going out with a girl with no arms or legs? You'll end up being a nursemaid to her. I didn't bring you up to be a nursemaid."

It wasn't the first time I'd heard something like this but I felt gutted. I thought, this is a bad start. I couldn't carry on skulking behind the wall though so I pushed myself sheepishly out, using my crutches under my arms, and she and I looked at each other.

She had an olive skin but as she took in the reality of me her face went totally white, like all the blood had drained away. It looked like she might faint. She said not a word to me except "Goodbye" and turned away. Later John told me that she had cried all the way home and kept asking him: "How could you go out with a girl like that? Why don't you call the girl you used to do ballroom dancing with, see if you can go out with her again?"

She tried everything to persuade him to go out with this girl or some other. Anyone but me, in other words, but he didn't want to. I learned later that she got so agitated about me she started taking sleeping tablets.

As for me, the way she looked at me had made me feel terrible but I had known what to expect so I was not exactly taken by surprise. I'd got used to going after what I wanted, what nurtured me and made me feel good, without worrying what anyone else thought of me, so I told myself, well, I'm going out with her son and she's either going to have to get used to it or not.

For John's sake, and because I really wanted to get to know her, I did make a big effort over a long period to encourage her to see beyond my disabilities. I wanted her to get to know me, to see the Louise that John loved. He knew that I had no arms or legs but because his eyes were so bad he didn't rely on physical appearance to judge people. He had the ability to go beyond that to the personality and spirit underneath and it was that he had fallen for in me.

After we had been going out for a few months, John and I decided to go on our first holiday together to Benidorm. It cost £79 for the two of us for two weeks, which we thought was a great bargain. The reason it was so cheap was that we had to travel from Cheltenham to Bristol on a National Express coach, then from Bristol to Benidorm in another coach.

It took 72 hours and it was awful. Every time I wanted to

go to the loo, John had to get my wheelchair out of the luggage hold, lift me off the coach, push me to the ladies and wait for me, then chuck me back on the coach and stow my wheelchair away again. We were at the front which meant I could lie down comfortably across two seats as they made just the right sized bed for me but every time the driver braked, I rolled over and fell off. So John slept on the seat on the other side and stretched his legs across the way to rest his feet on my shoulders so that when the coach slowed down, he could hold me steady. We travelled that way all the way to Benidorm.

When we got off the coach at our hotel we took our stuff upstairs, locked our travellers' cheques in the safe and went down to dinner. John is a true Englishman in the sense that his take on foreign food is: forget it. He took one look at the omelettes and paella and went "yuk". Nearby we spotted a chicken and chips place so we toddled off there, then we fancied a drink and went looking for a nightclub.

We were only young, 19 or 20, and we wanted to party all night in true Spanish style. We soon found an all-night disco where we danced and laughed and had a few drinks. Quite a few drinks, in fact, so by the time we left there in the early hours we were both absolutely gone.

As we were giggling our way back to the hotel we had to go past a row of shops with a frontage which stayed on one level while the road next to it sloped down. Somehow, I got the right wheel of my chair on the frontage and the left on the road. John couldn't see what was happening because it was dark and I didn't realize I was slowly tipping sideways because I was drunk. So neither of us was expecting it when I finally toppled over, hit the deck and cut my eye on the pavement.

On the coach the tour guide had made a big thing of warning us: "Whatever you do, keep an eye on your handbag," as there were thieves about and, as I lay in the gutter, this was all I could think about. So I started yelling, "Oh, my handbag, my handbag," and an old lady who had been sitting in her doorway across the road, came steaming over, convinced John was mugging me, and bashed him over the head with her handbag.

As we couldn't speak a word of Spanish, nor she English, it took some time for us to persuade her to stop. Despite our pleas, she called the police who summoned an ambulance which took me all of 200 yards to the hospital where I had six stitches in my eye then took me back to the hotel and demanded instant payment of £100. As we had only taken £200 for the whole two weeks, this made something of a dent in our pile of travellers' cheques which I had to get out of the safe and sign even though I still wasn't at all coherent.

I remember waking up at about midday the next day lying on my front, realizing how hot it was in my room and that my head was pounding. I groaned, "Oh my God, what happened?" John said, "Don't you remember?" and sat me up in front of the mirror. As I took in the full horror of my face, I yelped and jumped back. My right eye was as black as the ace of spades, there was blood still in my hair. I looked an absolute state.

Still, nothing was going to stop us enjoying ourselves so as soon as we felt better we headed for the bar where we made friends with a couple from Yorkshire who were on holiday with their daughter and grandchildren. This turned out to be lucky for them because a few days later the grandson, who was aged about 12, decided to jump the concrete pillars in front of the hotel. He landed on one, slipped off and broke his leg, so he was plastered up and had to spend the rest of the fortnight on crutches. This made it very hard for him to get to the beach about quarter of a mile away so I said he could use my chair in the mornings while I was sleeping off the revels of the night before. He took it at 9 a.m. and brought it back at 12. He really appreciated that.

John and I spent the afternoons on the beach where I sunbathed in my bikini. I had deliberately searched out the brightest and tiniest bikini I could find; it was coloured red, yellow and blue and was a little triangle of cloth for the bottom half and a couple of tiny triangles for the top, held together with strings. And I wasn't exactly the smallest girl on the beach. I was probably stared at, but I didn't care because I was with John and he loved me and I loved him to bits. We were just really happy together.

A year later we went to Majorca for Christmas with John's parents – we flew this time. There was a dressing-up competition in the hotel so the rest of them got me up as a Smurf. They painted my face blue, put a new Christmas jumper on me and a crepe paper hat. As Momma Smurf I won the contest and collected two bottles of champagne for the family.

We had a great time but John's mother still didn't like me and after he left the Queen Elizabeth College she made one last effort to break us up. At first he lived at home and worked for his father, a haulage contractor, during the week and came to stay with me at weekends, then after I left college he moved in with me permanently.

He had been with me a few weeks when his mother phoned him and told him she wanted him to come home. He refused so she said, "If you don't, I'm going to have your dog put down." His dog was a beautiful German Shepherd called Kitchener which he adored. This was plain blackmail but he couldn't bear the thought of losing his dog so he caved in and went home.

He was there for a month and he was miserable. He phoned me every night at 8 p.m. for an hour, telling me how much he missed me. One day his mum said to him, "You aren't happy, are you? Go back to her then." She rang me to tell me she was bringing him back and when they got here she sat on the settee and said to me, "Louise, John's been really unhappy. I've tried to give him everything but the one person he is missing is you."

Though my relationship with John's mother was difficult, I had a lot of respect for her and over the years I learned vital lessons from her which I was very grateful for. Growing up at Chailey meant I never learned about the unwritten rules which make family life work. So when I went to her house or she came to ours, I observed her and I copied the things she did, the routine she used, and that was how I learned to run a household.

John and I lived together for two years and were really happy but by the summer of 1986 I wanted to move things on. I wanted to have children, we had been talking about it for some time and I didn't want to have them outside marriage. I wanted security and I really loved John and everyone kept asking when we were going to get engaged, so I put a little pressure on him.

I said to him one day, "We're not going anywhere, either we've got to make this more permanent or things have got to change," and I asked him if he'd marry me. He said "yes" and the next day, really excited, I rang my mum and dad to tell them. They were pleased but cautious. Dad said, "Just be happy with the engagement at the moment."

Feeling a bit dampened, we decided to leave it a while before we officially got engaged. That Christmas we went to John's sister's who had just had a baby. On Christmas Day I was sitting on the settee with the baby and John got down on his knees beside me and said, "Louise, will you marry me?"

I could not have been happier, I loved him so much, and we started planning the perfect wedding. I decided I wanted to walk up the aisle because for once I wanted to be the same height as him and it meant I could wear a full length wedding dress. It would turn out to be the last time I would ever wear my artificial legs.

I had used them on and off since I left college but I found that outside of institutional life the legs were a pain. It would take me ages to get anywhere and if anyone brushed past me or I tripped over a stone, I would crash to the ground like a falling tree and hurt myself. On top of that, I had no real need for them as I could get about efficiently in my chair. The legs I had made me taller than John at 5ft 6ins so I rang Roehampton and they agreed to make me a shorter pair. I had to be able to stand for the whole of the wedding so they made them a tight fit.

When it came to choosing the dress I found a company in Gloucester that brought dresses to your home and my mother decided she wanted to help me make the selection. The relationship between my mum and me has always been somewhat strained and this occasion was no exception though it was a nice time too.

A lady came and hung the dresses up around my living room. My mum had definite ideas of what kind of wedding dress I should have, which was a short one. I said I wanted a long dress with a train. She said it should be a short train, I said I wanted a long one. We went on for quite a while like that until she picked out a long dress which I liked – very low-cut with lots of frills round the neck and three quarter sleeves which could be taken up at the shoulder to make them shorter – and I chose a tiara.

The wedding was set for June 20, 1987 at St Andrews church in Totteridge, North London, near my family's house. Two days beforehand I went to stay there with Nicky who was to be my maid of honour, and we visited the hairdresser, who was the daughter of my dad's chauffeur, to show her what she would have to work with.

The day of the wedding was absolutely extraordinary. First of all, I didn't want to get out of bed because I was having the best time I'd ever had at home, being fussed over by my mum and dad and my sisters. It was like I was truly part of the family, something I hadn't felt for a long time. I was the centre of attention but it wasn't that I was enjoying so much, it was the feeling of actually being wanted. I almost didn't want to get married because it would bring that feeling to an end.

Finally, I hauled myself out of bed and Nicky washed my hair in beer shampoo because it supposedly gave it a lot of shine. I don't know if it did that but I know I stunk of beer. I had breakfast, had my hair set by the hairdresser and my make-up done by my Aunt Hilary who worked as a BBC make-up artist.

Nicky helped me put my legs on and get into my dress, then Dad knocked on the door to tell me the cars had arrived. I came out of my bedroom in my dress with the veil down and flowers decorating my crutches and saw my dad waiting for me. His face was great, he was grinning from ear to ear. I could see he was really proud of me and I felt wonderful. My mum's face was wreathed in a great big beam too and so were my sisters'.

Nicky and the chauffeur helped me into the vintage car. My veil was a bit long and was spread on the seat and when my dad got in he sat on it so my head was pulled at an angle all the way to the church. But it was only five minutes so it was OK.

On the way he said to me, "Now don't rush up the aisle, you don't want to trip over, it will spoil your day if you fall over as you go up the aisle." He got me out of the car, we met up with the four small children who were my maids and pages and then we set off up the aisle with my dad still whispering, "Don't rush, keep it slow, be careful you don't fall over. I'll be here to catch you if you do."

What was going through my mind was, what happens if my knee lock breaks? What if I fall in front of all these smiling people? The wedding was being filmed for the TV programme World in Action and there were lots of press there too so I would have humiliated myself in front of millions of viewers and newspaper readers as well as the congregation if I'd gone flat on my face.

Then I saw John waiting for me at the altar and I forgot all my worries. He was biting his nails and he looked a bit hung-over but he was so smart and handsome in his wedding suit. I didn't focus on the congregation or the TV cameras or his mum who was wearing a bright turquoise suit with a great big blue hat, any more, I just focused on John. And when I reached him he turned round and said, "I love you."

It was a fabulous wedding except that John and I had our first argument at the altar. We were singing "Jerusalem" and when I sing I have a very loud voice so he poked me in the ribs telling me I was making far too much noise. At the end of the service, everybody clapped, which was amazing. We walked through the congregation arm in arm and it was his turn to keep whispering, "Go slowly, you don't want to fall over."

The reception was for about 120 people at a country club just down the road from home. By the time the speeches came I had been wearing my legs for about five hours and they were getting really tiresome so I was very glad to take them off and change into my going-away outfit. I threw my bouquet which was caught by my sister Lindsey, then we got in my dad's car and his chauffeur drove us to Gatwick where we spent our wedding night in a hotel.

The next morning we flew off to Florida for our

honeymoon in Disneyworld, which was great as America was so far ahead of Britain at that time in facilities for the disabled. The whole holiday was out of this world. John was so perfect in those days and we had a lot of laughs.

Once in Disney village he had forgotten to bring his passport which, because he looked so young, he needed to prove that he was old enough to drink, i.e. over 21. He wanted a lager but the waiter refused to believe his age so I had to go up to the bar to order it. When the waiter came he put the beer in front of me and the Coke I wanted in front of John. We had to sit side by side to confuse him over who was drinking what.

For most of our marriage John and I got on fantastically well. We did everything together and went all over the place. We bought a caravan and used to go away for weekends to small, friendly caravan sites in fields in picturesque places and we took holidays in Benidorm, Miami, and Tenerife.

I came off the pill on the day we got back from our honeymoon and two weeks later I was late for my period. I couldn't believe I could have conceived so quickly but I couldn't wait to find out so I rushed off to the chemist's, got a kit and did the test. The two minutes I had to wait for the result seemed like for ever but I was ecstatic when the blue line appeared which showed that I was pregnant.

I rang John at work to tell him and he was totally shocked. He said, "No, you can't be! It's only been two weeks." When I showed him the proof later he reacted the way you would always hope a man would – he was celebrating, happy, excited and proud. He rang his mum and she was really happy too.

Then I rang my mum and she was not so forthcoming. The first thing she said was: "Don't tell anyone yet. It's too early, you might lose it and you don't know for definite that you are pregnant anyway until you have a proper test at the doctor's."

I said, "I know I am," and she said, "No, you don't, Louise. You've never been pregnant before."

I took her advice and redid the test at the family planning clinic. It came out the same but my mum said I should still keep it quiet for four months in case something happened.

Then I rang my G.P. and told him I was pregnant and he said, "Is that a good thing?" I was so shocked and upset by his unsupportive attitude that I rang the General Medical Council in Cheltenham and told them I wanted to change my doctor.

My new doctor was much better. He said he would have to make sure he monitored me properly but I told him the only difference between me and any other pregnant woman was that I had no arms and legs. What was the big deal when I had all the bits that a baby actually needs? I wasn't apprehensive about how I would manage because I had spent a great deal of time thinking it all through. I sadly accepted that there were things I would never be able to do, like bathing the baby, and that for safety reasons I would need a nanny, but I worked out ways of doing most things myself.

For instance, I decided to breast feed and experimented over how to do it by messing around at home. I reckoned that if I lay sideways on the bed with a pillow next to me, I could put the baby on it and we would both be quite safe and comfortable.

During my pregnancy one of the doctors I saw asked me what I would do if my child was born disabled. I bristled and snapped, "If there is anything wrong, I am more qualified to look after it than you are. And there's one thing for sure, whatever the problems, it will be brought up at home." In fact we could see on the scan that our baby was a girl with a full set of arms and legs so we were more concerned in case her eyes were like John's though we knew how to cope with that too.

I loved being pregnant and had no morning sickness. Emma used to kick between 8 and 9 in the morning, 3 and 4 in afternoon and 8 and 10 at night, so I would make sure I was lying down at those times so she would have room to move around in.

I was only the second four-limbs deficient Thalidomider to have a baby so no one had much experience about how I would manage giving birth. The hospital told me I would need a caesarean because I had weak pelvic floor muscles but I wanted to do everything as naturally as I could. I persuaded them that, if everything was going OK, they should let nature take its course.

In the event Emma decided to arrive four weeks early. John was in the pub where he used to go every night from 10 to 11.30 when I started having contractions. I rang the maternity services, told them my name, said I was due in a month's time and was having contractions every ten minutes. The nurse said I should lie back and relax.

I phoned John and he said that if the hospital says relax, that's what I should do. As soon as I put down the phone, it rang and it was the nurse suddenly sounding a lot less relaxed. She said, "We've just looked at your records. You're special needs, we had better get you in. We are sending an ambulance."

John came haring back with a pint in his hand and said, "If you get to hospital and it's a false alarm, I shall be very cross." I thought, I hope the contractions don't stop because I don't want him to be cross.

When I got there they put me on a monitor and the contractions stopped. John was sent home and I had a really peaceful night before they started again at 6 a.m. and John was called back. It was decided I should have a caesarean that day, April 14, 1988 and I chose to have an epidural so I could stay awake. I didn't want to have carried her for eight months and then to miss the best bit.

John was there holding my hand when I had the injection and he went really white and then green, and the nurse told him to go out. He didn't want to come into the delivery room which was probably a good thing too as he didn't cope well with blood. So I was on my own as I watched the doctor lift Emma out, cut the umbilical chord and put her on my chest and, oh, it was an experience you can never, ever describe. There are no words that could even come close. It was really heart-warming. I murmured "hello" to her and they weighed her, four and a half pounds. She was perfect and so beautiful. I cried.

They went out to tell John, who was standing smoking beside an oxygen cylinder, that he had a baby girl and he was so excited. We had already decided on a name so he rang everybody up to tell them Emma had arrived then rushed out to buy enough flowers to fill my whole room.

My parents came over later the same day and were overwhelmed with joy. I could see my dad giving Emma the love he wished he could have given me and I was pleased to see that happen. I wasn't jealous. It was too late for me but not for her. John's parents also came over straight away and were thrilled as well. Everyone made a huge fuss of us and we could not have been happier.

I stayed in hospital for two weeks learning how to feed and care for Emma. At her first feeding time a nurse brought her to me and she suckled but nothing came out. They wanted to give her a bottle but I refused to let them take her. I was determined to succeed so I tried again and this time it worked. We were bonded, she was mine and nothing was ever going to come between us.

She was kept in the special care baby unit for two days except when they brought her to me every feeding time and then she was allowed to be with me all the time. She was in my room and it was about midnight when she began to cry. I pressed the button for a nurse to come and told her she needed her nappy changing and she was hungry. She changed the nappy then went to take her away. I said, "Why are you taking her away?" and she said she was taking her down to nursery to feed her.

I said, "No, she's mine. I breast feed her." She said, "No, no. We are going to do it this week." I kicked up a real stink, it was around the time babies were being kidnapped from hospitals and I was very anxious. Emma was crying her eyes out, I was getting into a real state but I felt utterly powerless and humiliated. It was the only time in my life that I was able to do nothing to get round my disability. It was the worst feeling ever. The nurse ignored all my pleadings and took her away. I cried all night and the next day the midwife asked me what was wrong. When I told her she went up to the nurse and said, "What did you do? Why isn't Emma with her mum? That was the worst thing you could have done."

The nurse was severely reprimanded and later came to

apologise to me. But I was still totally furious. I said, "I don't care. You wouldn't do that to any other mum, why do it to me?"

I'd already got a baby carrier which I wore on my front and that was how I held her. After her feed I rocked her to sleep in the carrier then they took her out and put her in the cot.

On the day we were to come home, John fetched us in a Rolls Royce. He had had the garden specially done and had strung balloons all the way down the drive, filled the house with flowers and bought champagne. Despite feeling a bit car-sick as I rode along in the Rolls – just as I had done in my father's Rolls when I was little – it was all lovely and I was blissfully happy. John was the perfect dad.

For the first two weeks at home I had an Australian maternity nurse who helped me figure out the best way of doing things. That was one of the most contented periods John and I ever had, bonding with Emma, learning from the nurse and settling the baby into her routine. When Emma cried in the night for her feed we had an intercom so both the nurse and I heard her and we both got up. I arranged my pillows, the nurse picked her up, changed her nappy, gave her to me and latched her on. Emma usually fell asleep at the breast and the nurse burped her and put her down. It worked fine.

The nurse was then replaced by a nanny whom John had hired while I was in hospital, called Michelle, and everything changed. Every time Emma cried, Michelle picked her up and cuddled her, trying to soothe her back to sleep herself instead of bringing her straight to me. It was so frustrating and upsetting not being able to pick up my own baby when she cried and having to rely on someone else who would not do what I asked.

I got really uptight about this so when Nicky was here one day and Michelle started cuddling Emma I said, "Michelle, can I have Emma," and she said, "No. I'm cuddling her." Nicky was really cross to see this so she went to Michelle's room and told her, "This is Louise's baby." Michelle stomped in and bad-temperedly thrust Emma at me. After I'd fed her and Nicky had left I said to Michelle, "Emma is mine, not yours. If she cries, it's me that says what goes on."

This sense of powerlessness and vulnerability because you can't take physical control of a situation is the most difficult thing for someone like me. I felt a bit better, more in control, for a couple of days, but then similar things started happening again. I didn't know what to do because I couldn't manage without a nanny and didn't want to have to start all over again with a new one so soon. John said I was being paranoid and that it was just my hormones playing up.

A couple of days later Michelle's previous employer rang up and said they had been looking for her for a month. They told me they had left their toddler with her while they went away and when they came back he wouldn't come out from under the table. They took his nappy off and found hand marks on his bottom and when they confronted her she had disappeared and social services were looking for her.

I was shocked. Who was this person who I was allowing to care for my precious baby? I told Michelle she must either go immediately to social services and clear her name or leave. She packed her bags and left, much to my relief. Instead, John's mum came to look after me and Emma for a week which was even more awful. She didn't just take over like Michelle had done but acted as if I wasn't wanted on the scene at all. In her eyes, Emma was John's baby, not John and Louise's baby. It was pretty odd.

Thankfully, we soon hired another nanny who stayed for three or four months. She was fine, we got into a routine and Emma started rolling over and sitting up. If she had a babygro on I could bite that, lift her up and carry her around with my teeth. I could also carry her on my shoulder until she got to 6-7 months.

But there were many times when she cried and I couldn't pick her up, when she was on the floor, too low down for me to reach with my teeth, or had got too big, and I felt terribly helpless. The thing I longed to do most was to bath her. I felt I really missed out on doing that. Once when she was a bit older she said to me, "Mummy, bath me," and I told her gently, "I'm sorry, I can't. I can put you in the bath and I can sit and play with you when you are in it, but I can't get you out." Those are special times, getting your baby out of a bath, wrapping her in a towel, when a mum gets that closeness with her child and it's lovely. I did resent the carers for doing that instead of me but, even though it hurt, I had to do what was best and safest for Emma.

When that nanny left we decided to advertise for a local mother's help and over the next few years we employed a stream of them, some good, some bad, all very young. It was very hit and miss. As Emma began to toddle around, I decided to get an electric wheelchair instead of using the manual one propelled by my crutches, so that I could take her out safely by myself. I had adaptations made – a footplate for her to stand on, a bar across to keep her in and something in the middle to stop her slipping down. It worked great. I trundled along for miles in that chair with her riding in front and our two dogs trotting beside us.

Chapter Eight
Sadness And Hurt

Two years after Emma was born I got pregnant again but one day in the early stages my wheelchair tipped up, I fell out and I miscarried which messed up my hormone system and I didn't have another period for about eight months. Two days after Emma's second birthday we moved out of our comfortable home in Cheltenham to a two-bedroom council bungalow while we had the house extended, adding a bedroom and toilet upstairs and extending the kitchen and our bedroom and bathroom. John and I, with Emma and the dogs, were in one bedroom, the mother's help in the other and there was a tiny little kitchen and living room where the dogs slept. It was oppressive and awful but it was only supposed to be for four months.

It ended up being six months by which time we were pulling our hair out. John was working at a haulage depot and would leave the house at 6 a.m. and might not get back till midnight. I couldn't get out anywhere except to walk the dogs because this place was on the other side of Cheltenham so I felt lonely and isolated and under a lot of strain. I found myself sinking into a depression, not just because of our difficult living conditions but more to do with the fact that having a baby brings all kinds of suppressed emotions to a head. I loved Emma so much that the question nagged at me more and more until it became an obsession: How could my mother have given me up?

Before you have your own child you think it must be easy,

that it might hurt for a couple of days but you would get over it. But when I had Emma I realised, you can't give a baby up. I had such an incredibly strong bond with Emma and it wasn't something I had to think about. It was natural, it was there. So I wondered how could my mum and dad cut that bond? And when they did, how painful was it? Also, I'm not very good at being cooped up with other people and at that time I had a carer I wasn't particularly getting on with. Plus I had two dogs in our bedroom as well as Emma. It got to the point where I just couldn't cope. I was on the verge of a nervous breakdown.

The stress of all this bubbling under the surface found its physical expression in me having my hair cut off. I needed to shout but I couldn't shout out loud. I was confined to these small rooms, cut off from people and, subconsciously, I needed to do something that people would see so they would take notice. John liked long hair and used to enjoy playing with mine and putting it up, so when he came home and saw that I had got the hairdresser to cut it all off, leaving a crew-cut just two inches long, he knew something was seriously wrong. He called the doctor and told him he thought I needed to see a psychiatrist. I agreed because I couldn't understand why I was feeling so bad.

I saw the psychiatrist every other week for five months and talking everything over with him did me good. Together we worked it out that my emotional distress went right back to when my grandpa died and I didn't have chance to say goodbye because I was very close to him, closer than to my parents, so when I lost him I had nothing left. My mum and dad were blood parents but not the kind of people I could relate to. I had cooped up that hurt in a box and basically the box was full and I couldn't release it.

I was nine years old when it happened in January, 1972. I was feeling pretty weak as I was getting over a bout of scarlet fever which had been followed by shingles when one night I had a dream about my grandpa and that he came to say goodbye to me. I woke up crying and, when asked what was wrong, I couldn't say as I felt stupid because it was only a dream. I got up and dressed, put my legs on and went down to breakfast as usual. Then the telephone rang and I knew it was about me. Sister Myers, who was in charge of Junior Dorm where I was living at the time, asked me to come to her office and told me that my grandpa had died at home at six that morning and I should go to school and have a good day.

I walked to school crying. I told no one, I just went on as usual. After all, nobody else cared. I wasn't even invited to Grandpa's funeral so I had always felt I had never had a chance to say goodbye, except in my dream. It haunted me for years and still hurts. It made me hard. I cried very little after this, but beneath the tough exterior, my feelings of hurt, loss and bewilderment had been building up ever since and the psychiatrist helped me lay them to rest.

However, he didn't reconcile me to my past completely: there were still lots of questions I wanted to ask my parents. I tried to put myself in their position and ask myself how I would have felt if Emma was disabled and I was able-bodied. I understood in a sense how difficult it must have been for them and what a shock it must have been in the days before scans. My mother wasn't expecting anything to be wrong and it must have been an absolute nightmare. Yet I still found it very hard to accept completely. Years later I asked my dad whether, if it happened now, would he do the same thing over again, would he still put me in Chailey, and to my shock and horror, he said "yes". I guess I'll never fully understand.

Once I had recovered and we were back in our house which now had a nice room and bathroom for the mother's help upstairs, John and I were keen to have another baby. My periods had still not returned properly so I went to the doctor who gave me tablets to give me a kick start. He told me to take them for three days then wait ten days and in the meantime to be as promiscuous as possible. After ten days I still hadn't started so I rang the doctor who said that either the tablets had not worked or I was pregnant. This was a possibility that hadn't occurred to me but just to be sure I got a pregnancy test which, to my amazement, came out positive. When I took Emma to playschool the next day on my wheelchair I asked her how she would like a baby brother or sister and she said,

"Oh, yeah!" That evening after tea John was sitting watching TV with Emma next to him and she piped up, "Daddy, Mummy's going to have a baby."

She showed him the test and he went wild with delight again, just like the first time. He was happy, he was proud. It was something we both wanted and he treated me like royalty so for a while the stress we had been under disappeared. Unlike with Emma, this time I had a lot of sickness but in the evening rather than the morning so to conquer it I ate my evening meal in the morning and my breakfast in the evening.

On top of the sickness, I had cysts on my kidneys which were getting worse and giving me a lot of pain. I inherited polycystic kidneys from my mother and it has always seemed to me a particularly cruel irony that I should be inflicted with that through my genes when I am already severely disabled through a condition that has nothing to do with my DNA. Eight weeks before Jack was due one of the cysts burst and I was in excruciating pain. People kept telling me to take painkillers but I refused. I had a total phobia about swallowing any kind of tablet while I was pregnant, not surprisingly.

A fortnight later another really big cyst burst and I was in so much pain I thought I was going to die. Though I still had six weeks to go, I really couldn't bear it any longer so I began to push Jack out. They took me to hospital and gave me an injection to stop the contractions then did a caesarean. When it was over I finally, and gratefully, swallowed the painkillers.

Jack was born on February 26, 1992 and despite his rough start in life, he was fine and I was besotted all over again. They kept him in the special care baby unit for a while but brought him to me for feeds. I was a dab hand at managing breast feeding by then and everything went well until one night not long before we were due to go home.

They gave him formula milk in the nursery which resulted in him getting bad colic. After that he took ages to feed and would scream with pain and he didn't sleep through the night until he was two.

My maternal instincts were extremely powerful but I still had to learn a lot about how to care for my children because

I'd been brought up in an institution where the individual nourishing that only a mother gives was missing. I learned so much from carefully observing John's mother and also by watching the way my animals cared for their babies. One thing that was always clear from the beginning was that babies don't see what you look like and don't care how many arms or legs you have, you are their mum. When I took Emma to the mother and toddlers group the other kids would ask, "Where's your mum?" and she would point me out.

One day she was rather quiet and I realised it was time I explained things to her. I said, "Do you know why Mummy is like she is? It's because Mummy's mummy was given a bad tablet when Mummy was inside her and it stopped her arms and legs growing." I've always been a great believer that if you tell kids the truth they have got something they can say to defend themselves against all the bickering. As they got older I gave them more and more information and Emma can now tell you exactly in fairly fine detail why I am like I am.

Both she and Jack always stuck up for me. A child once said to Emma, "My mummy can hug me," and Emma said, "Well my mummy can hug me too but in a different way. Your mummy puts her arms round you and holds you. With my mummy, I put my arms round her and she grabs hold of my shoulder." And she added, "Either way, my mummy still loves me."

I was careful to bring them up to be no different from other children. I had got used to doing things like turning the lights on and off with my head and holding a pencil in my mouth to write and, inevitably, Emma started copying me. We used to sit at the kitchen table colouring and she was doing hers with the colouring pencils in her mouth. I told her to use her hand but she said, "You do it like this," so I realised I would have to stop. Not that it was a bad thing to do it with your mouth but she would soon be going to nursery school and she didn't need to be picked on for colouring with her mouth. So I got the mother's help to do the colouring so she would copy her. It was hard for me to sit by and watch them but eventually Emma turned the lights on and off and drew using her hand and that was best for her.

Both children sensed that the carers were there to do all the things Mummy couldn't do but carers came and went and the only person who was there all the time was me. If they fell over, they always ran to me and I'd give them a magic kiss. Only Mummy's magic kiss would work.

There was just one carer that both Emma and I got on particularly well with. She became almost a second mum and when she left Emma took it really badly so I told her, "You mustn't get too close to carers. You must keep a distance. They will always go, there is nothing to keep them here, but I will always be here." She kept more of a distance after that and she told Jack to do the same though it was not so much of a problem with him. Jack was a typical boy, always by my side, wanting to be with his mum and very, very loving.

Though I was ecstatically happy and busy with my two gorgeous children, taking them to mother and toddlers group and later to nursery, my relationship with John began to go downhill. He was great at playing with the children, making them laugh and changing their nappies when they were babies but he found it extremely hard to be both a husband and a carer to me.

The mother's help would have every other weekend off and he would have to fill in. He didn't like having to wake up at 8 a.m. on Saturday morning but babies don't know what time it is and Emma would always wake at 8 a.m. on the dot and demand to be fed. John would get grumpy and I hated having to badger him and resented being forced to do it. The strain was building up so I had to get another carer to cover the weekends too but it didn't make things much better.

When Jack was nearly two we decided to go to Lanzarote for Christmas and asked the mother's help we had at the time, if she would come with us. We rented a two-bedroom bungalow and all had a lovely time though the carer seemed rather shy as she refused to put shorts on and show her legs when sunbathing.

On New Year's Eve we all went to a nearby hotel for dinner, had a fantastic evening and saw the New Year in. Then

John said there was a nightclub up the road, the biggest in Lanzarote, and he would like to go but it was not wheelchair accessible. So I looked after kids and he went with the carer. The next day she appeared on the beach in a pair of shorts, though I didn't think anything of it at the time.

When we got home John announced that he was not going to sleep with me any more. He said I had put on weight and until I lost it he was sleeping upstairs in the spare room. I was distraught and immediately went on a crazy diet and lost about a stone and a half in four weeks but it didn't make any difference.

I trusted John not to betray me but I had a very strong feeling that something was not right. I started suspecting he was messing around and confided my fears in my cleaner, Sue, who had been coming to me for years and was a very good friend. She convinced me nothing was happening but I grew ever more anxious and depressed.

John agreed to go with me to Relate for marriage guidance. Nothing seemed to be wrong but the feeling persisted. I kept badgering and badgering him: "Are you sure there is nothing wrong? Are you seeing someone else?" After about ten days of this he finally said, "Yes, I'm seeing someone else, but I am not telling you who."

I was getting desperate, so I hired a private detective who followed him after work for three days and reported back that he was not going anywhere to see anyone. I didn't believe him, and I had to know. I thought, right, I know how to stop this once and for all.

I went through the Lady magazine and, without telling John, I found a cottage to rent during the Easter holidays in a tiny hamlet with just a pub and a shop in the middle of nowhere in Devon, thinking that whoever it was would not be able to get on a train and follow us down there. I asked the carer to pack the bags and when John came home from work at 6 p.m. everything was ready. She and the kids were in the car and the house was locked. When he appeared, I said, "Get in the car, we're going on holiday," and we drove off, not giving him enough time to phone anyone.

We got to the cottage and after we had put the children to bed I said to John, "Do you fancy going down the pub?" and he said that would be good. My whole aim was to find out who he was going with and one thing I knew about John was that when he had a few drinks he couldn't help telling the truth.

So I went to the bar to get the drinks and I slipped a vodka into his beer. By the time he had three of those he was getting pretty tipsy and I seized the moment. I said, "I want to know the truth. Who are you seeing?" At first he refused to cough up but as I kept on he eventually said, "If I tell you, will you promise not to go mad and show me up in this pub?"

I promised so he said, "Ok, I'm seeing the carer." I must have gone as white as a sheet. My heart broke, just like that. It all suddenly fitted into place, even the niggling feeling I'd had over her appearing in shorts on New Year's Day – the first time they had had sex was when they went to that nightclub together on New Year's Eve and afterwards she didn't feel shy about showing her legs any more.

I finished my drink, feeling sick. John said nervously, "Had we better go back?" When we got to the little cottage she opened the door and I ran my wheelchair straight into her legs and called her every name under the sun. I went into our room and started packing, screaming at her, "You've taken my husband, take my kids too. I can't look after them. You've taken a big part of my life away." I was absolutely distraught. I put the dogs in the car and got in myself but before I could drive off John came and took the keys away, which was very sensible as I was in no fit state to go anywhere.

I had no alternative but to go to bed but didn't sleep a wink all night. The next day I had calmed down a bit and, trying to keep things normal for the kids, we all went to a reservoir for a walk. But I was still seething with rage and hurt and when we got out of the car I ran straight into her legs again. I kept on doing it.

John shouted, "Stop, you're upsetting the kids," and they kept asking, "What's wrong, Mummy?" I told him it was his fault they were upset. This obviously couldn't go on but the horrible thing was that I couldn't escape on my own. I couldn't manage without someone to help me.

So I dropped them off and went off in the car to use my mobile phone to ring the employment agency which had originally sent the carer, but it was Easter and they had no one to replace her. In desperation I got hold of Sue, my cleaner, who thankfully promised that she would come and look after me. I went back to cottage and told the carer she was sacked then packed everything up and got everyone in the car. When we got back to Cheltenham I needed help getting out of the car. John and the carer got the kids out then John said, "Don't help her out. She sacked you, you don't have to help her now." So she didn't. She just left me there.

I rang Sue who said she would be there in 20 minutes. For a while I sat in the car, but then I couldn't stand it any more being left, marooned there in the drive. I wriggled out of the car, opened the gate and started crawling down the road. You do mad things when you are completely devastated.

John realised what was happening, came running out of the house and picked me up. He lugged me back to the car, shoved me in and locked it. Luckily, soon afterwards Sue turned up and got me out. I had already phoned the carer's mum and told her that if she didn't come and get her within half an hour, I was calling the police so it wasn't long before she turned up, apologised for her daughter's actions and drove her away.

I came into the house where I found John looking furious. He said, "I will never forgive you for what you've done, never." I loved him so much that until that moment I had thought that with her out of the way I would forgive him so long as he promised not to do it again. But when he said that I burst into tears and went into the bedroom. Emma and Jack couldn't understand what was going on. They thought it was some kind of game so they poured shampoo over my head and started rubbing it in for a laugh. John was egging them on saying, "Good kids. You don't like Mummy either." It was horrible.

I managed to get myself together enough to feed Emma and Jack and put them to bed, then I lay down myself and cried for hours, absolutely bucketing down with tears. I knew my marriage had come to an end. My husband had cheated on me and he wasn't even sorry. The next day I realised I would have to get something sorted out but I wasn't likely to be able to get a replacement carer for at least ten days so I went down to Social Services, which really went against the grain because I never, ever asked them for anything.

But you do the things you have to do so I saw the duty officer and explained what had happened and she said I would have to see the duty social worker. Twenty minutes after I got home I got a phone call saying a man called Duncan Siret would come and see me. That turned out to be the beginning of a beautiful friendship, one of the most significant friendships of my life. At a time when I had lost all trust in men, Duncan was my knight in shining armour and made a huge difference to my life from the day he walked into it.

After I'd explained it all to him he said he wanted to see John too and would return when he got back from work at 6 p.m. That evening he read my statement out to John and asked him what he had to say about it and John said, "I want Louise to be put in a home. I'm not going to look after her and the kids don't need her. I can have the nanny back and she can help me look after them."

This was devastating for me to hear. Yet again it was someone who was supposed to love me who wanted to put me away in an institution. Duncan's mouth dropped in astonishment and he was having none of it. He said firmly, "We don't do that. We don't take a mum away from her kids unless she is endangering them." He added that as far as the children were concerned, John was their father and he was responsible for looking after them. John retorted, "I'll look after the kids but I'm not looking after her." It was obvious Duncan didn't like John's attitude so he said he would go away and think about it.

The next day he phoned to say he had found a nurse who could come temporarily to look after me and the children but not John, her name was Emma too. We got on really well and she ended up staying a month.

During that time it was my Emma's birthday and I'd arranged a party at McDonalds for her and her friends. John was still living at home but as the weeks went by the situation became unbearable because he was so nasty to me and kept rubbing my nose in his adultery. Every time I saw him he would go on about how he had been with the carer and was still seeing her. He would say terribly hurtful things like: "You are not a good mum, you are crap. I don't know why I married you. I'm going off with her to a hotel in London."

Around that time I discovered it wasn't the first time she had done this kind of thing. In fact it was the third time she had been employed by a family and had gone off with the husband and she was still only 19. For the sake of my own sanity I had to get John out of the house so I reluctantly told my dad what had happened and he got a solicitor involved who said that the only way I could get rid of him was to start divorce proceedings.

A date was for a hearing in London which we both had to attend. With his sight being so bad, it wasn't easy for John to get there so he asked me for a lift. I reluctantly said yes. It seems bizarre now that I took my husband to London to divorce him. I dropped him off round the corner so we wouldn't be seen arriving together.

In the divorce court he was very eloquent and seemed to turn everything round to be my fault but the court said he had to leave by May 27th. I helped him find a place and move in but when the time came for him to leave he was pretty upset and said he didn't want to go.

All his stuff was packed and he said to me, "Louise, I'm going. Please don't let me go. I promise I'll behave." I actually felt sorry for him as he was losing everything, his wife, his home, his children. I told myself it was his own doing and he was still seeing her but I don't think I would have been strong enough to resist his pleas if it wasn't for the fact I had promised my dad I would go through with it.

When I was growing up whatever my dad said went and I was still a little afraid of him, or at least, very anxious to please him. And I knew he would have gone loopy if I'd allowed John to stay.

A couple of weeks after John moved out I noticed he was looking really down in the dumps and asked what was wrong. He said he had just been to see her in the market in Swindon where she was working and had caught her with another man. He said to me, "You were right about her." I said, "Yeah." As soon as she had found out John had nothing, she had lost interest in him, but even though I was tempted to take him back, I didn't. It was too late for us.

I never wanted to be the kind of mother who stopped her children seeing their dad so I told John he could come and see them any time he wanted to. He got into the habit of stopping by for half an hour every evening after work. Sometimes he would come to stay to look after them but he would never take them out for the day.

As my kidney problems got worse I became so ill I couldn't cope with teenage tantrums and misbehaviour and John was good at sorting things out and keeping the peace. During our marriage he changed from a really nice man to a horrible spoilt brat, then he moved into his own place and became selfish yet vulnerable.

But as time went on he went back to what he was at the beginning, a gentle, kind and caring person, the man I fell in love with. We got past being bitter and in a way I never stopped loving him. He's not always been the perfect dad, especially when it comes to paying maintenance, but he has helped raise the kids from a distance and we are good friends.

I also have to accept my own share of the blame for the breakdown of our relationship. I realise I am not always the easiest person to live with and I've thought a lot about how being brought up in an institution has shaped me.

At Chailey, if I didn't like a particular nurse who was helping me over something or other, I could ask another. I could pick and choose who I related to as a friend as well and if I didn't get on with Joe Bloggs, I could totally ignore him, there were hundreds of others to talk to. But in a family you can't do that, you have to learn to get on with each other. I didn't have that understanding of the unwritten rules of family life.

Also, I was brought up to get on with life and do everything independently and I've always had to be very determined about what I want. So I am fiercely independent, not physically, but in my attitudes and, though I don't mean it, it comes over that I like things my own way.

In family life, when you have an opinion you learn to compromise, whereas in Chailey, you weren't taught to compromise. You either had something or you hadn't and if you hadn't, you had to fight for it. That was survival, but it wasn't the best way to create a happy family.

Chapter Nine
Working Life

When I left the Star Centre in the summer of 1981 and moved into my house in September of that year I spent the first few months revelling in my new-found freedom, keeping crazy hours, coming and going when I liked, eating exactly what I wanted when I wanted it.

But once I'd got used to it I thought it was time I got a job and I was perfectly confident I would soon find one. I stopped talking on CB radio all night, adjusted my meals back to a normal routine and took myself off to the job centre to apply for an office job. The first one that came up was a car dealership in Cheltenham which wanted a receptionist. I went round there to check it out and noticed the reception was downstairs at the back and they had a switchboard I was familiar with so I knew I could do the job.

I filled in the application form, putting that I was disabled and in a wheelchair, and was invited for an interview. The people at first interview were very open and it went well. Their attitude was, so long as I could do the job and had a friendly disposition, that's all they wanted to know. I was invited for a second interview and I thought, great. I felt really positive about it.

But when it came to the second interview with more senior staff, I knew as soon as I got through the door that there was a problem. They asked nit-picking questions about how I would operate the system which was really very simple. A few days later I got a letter saying I hadn't got the job because they were moving the receptionist upstairs and there was no access for a wheelchair.

I was pretty gutted as the only thing preventing me getting the job was lack of access and it seemed very odd to me to have the receptionist of a car dealership upstairs. So I went to check whether they had really moved it, and they had. Nowadays that would count as discrimination. They either couldn't move it, or would have to make it accessible if they did.

I knew it was discrimination then; there was a hell of a lot of it about. You could walk into interviews and know instantly that when they saw a wheelchair, they saw nothing but problems. You could sense them seeing pound notes flying out of the window as they sat there thinking, if we employ her it will cost xxx to provide facilities, or, she won't be able to do it, even though my qualifications proved I was perfectly capable.

After that I applied for a hundred and one other jobs. Literally. Some said no straight away. Some said I would have got the job if only I had some experience. Some said no because you're disabled and we haven't the facilities. I thought, this is not on, and by this time I was getting really bored. I had a black-and-white cross collie dog called Boomer and a tortoiseshell cat called Tigger and I spent a lot of time playing with them but apart from that I had nothing to do all day and I was demoralised by all the rejections.

So I went to see the local disabled resettlement officer who suggested I go to a training college to improve my qualifications and experience. At first I groaned at the thought of attending yet another residential institution but it was only a four-month course and it seemed I had no alternative if I was ever to get any work. That's how I started at the Queen Elizabeth Training College in April, 1982, where I did a course in business studies and office management, for which I gained a distinction, and met John. I did a two-week work placement in Leatherhead as part of the course and got on so well they asked me to stay on, but I was just putting roots down in Cheltenham and wanted to get going with life in my new home.

With my qualifications under my belt I had more luck with my job applications. I spotted an advert in the paper for Endsleigh Insurance which specialised in services for students. I knew they had an anti-discrimination policy so I had a good chance but I got the disabled resettlement officer to ring up on my behalf anyway. As a disabled person, you always seem to have to have someone backing you up, like a guarantor to say, "Oh yes, this person can do this and that." They won't take your word for it by itself.

The job was temporary, from September to November, and on the evening shift which was the least popular but it paid lots more money. I was absolutely chuffed when I got it. I didn't tell my parents because we were not speaking at the time – they were still upset with me for wanting an independent life. Now I felt justified. I felt like a proper, independent grown up. I had my own place, I had got a job even though it was temporary – it was a start and meant experience on my c.v. It really gave me a boost.

The shift was 7 p.m. to 11 p.m. and I drove myself there and back in my specially adapted Mini. The way this worked was that the foot pedals were extended so they were almost at the same level as the car seat. Because my legs didn't reach the end of it, the seat was cut back to three quarter size so that I sort of perched on it to work the lengthened pedals. Luckily, I have enough strength in my legs to push the pedals.

The controls were like an electronic version of helicopter controls, so for steering I had a lever which I pushed to left or right. It used to make a real screeching racket every time I moved it, like someone playing the violin extremely badly. The gears were automatic so I just had a gear stick which was extended high enough for my hands to hit it on and off and all the other controls were microswitches on a little pad raised up to the height of my hands.

Getting in and out of the car was quite a performance which took a lot of effort. It was a Mini Clubman estate and I kept the back seats and the passenger seat folded down. To get out of the car I would hurl myself on to the back of the passenger seat then swivel round and sit myself up on the back seats. I used a crutch to push open the back doors then I had a hoist, like they use in hospitals, which I clipped on to my wheelchair. The hoist worked by a hydraulic pump operated by a handle like you get on fruit machines so I pumped the chair into an upright position, pushed it round so it was dangling off the back of the car, then released a button to let it down. If I aimed it right the chair would come down directly behind the car, then I hopped on to it, released the hoist, shut the doors and propelled myself off with my crutches.

The worst thing about it was that when it rained, the chair got wet as it sat at the back of the car before I hopped on. That was horrible. If I had jeans on, as I usually did, the back of my legs stayed wet all day because I was sitting on them so they got no chance to dry.

To get back in again I opened the car doors, put the wheelchair level, swung the hoist round to clip it on to the chair, pumped up the hoist, swung the chair into the car, and let it down then wriggled into the driver's seat. It used to take me probably ten minutes to get in the car and six or seven to get out on a good day. If I had somebody with me it was a lot easier as they got the chair in and out. On my own I had to go through the whole procedure at home as well.

Access at Endsleigh was no problem as I went in the back and there was a lift up to the floor where I worked and they had a disabled toilet. The job was to input all the information about the contents of students' rooms into a word processor and some of the things they put were hilarious. For instance there was a question: "Have you got a TV?" to which quite a lot answered, "Yes, but not here." Often they didn't tick either yes or no which made my job really difficult. Since then I have always been very careful to mark boxes with a clear X when I am filling in forms.

We had to input so many per night and if you didn't meet your target then after a couple of months you could be the one who was dropped. It was good fun: people were friendly and there was a bit of competition to see who could get the most done. One lady could speed type and did them three times faster than me. Once she finished she went home – it took her three weeks to realise that she was paid not for the work she had done but the hours she had worked, so after that when she finished her quota she stayed on to make us all tea.

Getting my first pay packet made me feel wonderful – I had made it. It was a brown envelope containing £45 in cash which was a lot to me because at that time it cost me £20 to pay for my food for the week with a bit left over to go to the pub. So £45 felt like riches; it meant I could live well and put a little bit away for a rainy day.

I spent some of my first pay on a bottle of wine and a taxi after work to a housewarming party thrown by Nicky, my first carer who was later to be maid of honour at my first wedding. When she lived with me and I spent a lot of time on CB radio, one of the people I used to talk to was Kelvin and one day we arranged an "eyeball" in the local pub. He and Nicky fell for each other and they have been married now for 27 years but then they had just moved into a house with Kelvin's friend, Clive, and his girlfriend.

Kelvin and Clive were motorbike fanatics, always greasy, a mess to say the least, while Nicky was very tidy, minimalistic, everything had its place, and she found it very difficult moving into this house with three people who didn't care. The night they had their party, I arrived at 11.30 p.m. and found they had a fire in the back garden and people were draped all over the floor, drunk. Coming in sober, I put a bit of life back into things and the party went on to about 3 a.m.

They had bought me a bottle of Baileys, my favourite tipple, and challenged me to drink it. Which I did, the whole bottle. In the taxi on the way home I managed to get on the seat but I had to travel backwards with my nose pressed up against the seat because I was too drunk to turn round. Back home I felt *so* ill. When I lay down the room was spinning and I spent the whole night throwing up. The next evening I had to go to work again though I still had a hangover.

By end of that first week I was completely exhausted. Though I had enjoyed it, it had been six hours a day of continually typing, plus pushing myself there and back. On the Saturday morning I just stayed in bed I was so, so tired, but at the same time I was incredibly proud, thrilled with myself that I had got a job and done it. After that, I thought I could do anything.

The job was extended to six months, then I joined the careers office of Gloucestershire County Council's education department as a switchboard operator. It didn't use my qualifications but in those days a job with the council was for life. If the job was redundant, they seconded you somewhere else. Also, if a better job came up you had more chance of getting it as an internal candidate. Anyway, I enjoyed answering the phone in a cheery voice, saying, "County careers service, can I help you?" When I got bored with that I used to vary it by adding greetings like "Merry Christmas!" or "Happy Easter!"

I got to the stage where I could do the job with great speed and efficiency. It could be upsetting when the A Level results were published and kids would come on crying, "I didn't get the results I needed!" My heart would break because I knew they had worked really hard and hadn't got grades high enough to go to university. I tried to console them before putting them through to the careers office.

The only problem there was that I hated my office manager who treated me like a child. For instance, to get to my car I had to go down a ramp and into the road a little and she stood at the window, watching me. When I arrived in the office she said, "You nearly killed yourself. A car could have come up the road and hit you." I said, "It should watch where it's going then, shouldn't it." After that she got a bit narked and anything she could possibly pick me up on, she would, like she would tick me off for saying "Merry Christmas" though she couldn't give me a good reason why I shouldn't.

Once I forgot my lunch and my carer brought it to me arriving five minutes before the lunch break began. The manager gave her a good telling off then cross-examined her about what I did at home, which was none of her business. She was horrible. Nobody else liked her either because she made everyone's life hell but I was an easy target so I got the brunt of it.

After three years they introduced an automated telephone system and my job went to a receptionist. They didn't think I looked good enough visually for when kids came in so they transferred me to work on equal opportunities monitoring for the education department, which meant I became one of the first employees in the county to work from home. They paid for a computer and phone line and part of my electricity.

I went to the offices on Mondays to get my work load and then would stay up most of the night until I had finished it. I took Tuesdays off and went back in on Wednesday for more work to last me the rest of the week. I worked the rest of Wednesday and Thursday and took Friday off. I loved it because I could choose my own hours, have a break if I wanted, go out in the sunshine, take the dogs for a walk.

After about 18 months I was seconded again to computer programming working on Oracle, what is now Teletext, on a service where council jobs and training opportunities were advertised. I worked on a squared screen and had to programme each of the squares to produce fancy graphics, which was laborious but interesting.

I also filled in and monitored school accident reports which I sometimes found very disturbing. I came across three stabbings, two overdoses and one hanging. There was also monitoring bruising on children and because I knew one of the schools involved it could be upsetting. But it was a connection to real life and I enjoyed it.

That job lasted about a year which meant I had worked for Gloucestershire County Council around six years altogether by Christmas, 1990, when Emma was two and a half. John's mum and dad decided to take the whole family to Disneyland for Christmas and two days before we set off I got a letter from the council saying I was being made redundant.

It appeared that they had to make cuts and they always started off with the people who were less visible, the homeworkers. I used to think that if you worked for the council you had a job for life and I also thought that I was in their quota for the number of disabled people the government told them they had to employ but it turned out they had another disabled person who was working in the office so they could afford to lose one.

I can't say I cared very much because I had a lot to juggle. As well as looking after Emma, John wanted my attention, it seemed to me all the time. Looking back, I can see he probably felt pushed out as in the morning I was seeing to Emma, then he went off to work and when he came back I was cooking dinner, feeding her and putting her to bed. When I had time to sit down, he went to the pub to get some human contact.

I thought that if I had a few more hours to spend with Emma during the day, it would give me more time with John in the evening. I went back to the twilight shift at Endsleigh for a little while but I missed Emma too much. I wasn't there when she went to bed and when she got up in the morning I was too tired to keep up with her. And three times a week she wasn't there in the day because she was going to nursery school. So I left there and didn't apply for another job because I found out I was pregnant with Jack. I didn't think I could manage with two small children and a job and on top of that my kidney problems began to flare up badly. I missed working, not so much for the money as the opportunity to see people besides the carer and the kids. Instead I started going to a mother and toddler group and took more walks with the kids and the dogs. I was involved in Access For All in Cheltenham as well as the Community Health Council. I was playing cribbage in the local pub, too, so I did have some outside interests.

By the time I might have been ready to start looking for another job, John and I were locked in our marriage problems but, though that was a miserable time, it did lead to an unexpected path which has brought me some of the happiest times of my life.

One day the mum of Emma's best friend at school told me she was taking her son to a new youth group just starting in Cheltenham called the Woodcraft Folk and asked me if Emma would like to come. The atmosphere in the house was horrible so I thought it was best to get her out and sent her along on a Wednesday evening.

When I went to pick her up, lo and behold who should be there but Duncan, my knight in shining armour from the social services, who was one of the leaders. He was a hippie type, in his late 30s with long hair, wearing a black denim jacket and blue jeans and he looked really gorgeous. Everyone at Woodcraft Folk was very friendly. It was founded in 1925 and it's like the Scouts and Guides in that there are weekly meetings and camping trips in the summer but the ethos is quite different. It's a progressive educational movement which tries to give its members an understanding of vital issues of the day like the environment, world debt and sustainable development.

At the meetings the children play a lot of co-operative games. We try to teach them to share and always think of others, to work together and look after each other. They can get badges but they are awarded more to reaffirm what we teach on sharing. We do camping, drama, debates and campaigns, as well as crafts, singing and dancing. There are a lot of international links. The aim is to develop their self-confidence and educate them about social change and getting involved in society to build a world based on equality, peace, social justice and co-operation.

As a kid I liked going to the Brownies, Cubs and Guides though I was kicked out of the Brownies because I was too mischievous. They sent me to the Scouts instead, hoping it would calm me down though I can't say it did. But I was even more drawn to the Woodcraft Folk and started going for a drink with them after the meeting, on warm Wednesday evenings. About a month after Emma joined they had their first camp which was for all the family but I couldn't go because Jack was just over a year old and starting to toddle around. I dropped Emma off and went back in the middle of the week to see how she was getting on.

Everyone was off on a walk and I spotted that one of the tents was falling down. Because I'd been in the Girl Guides I knew you shouldn't have ropes touching canvas but the ropes on this one were slack and trailing against the side of the tent. So I jumped out of my wheelchair, found a mallet on the floor and started banging the pegs in.

When Duncan came back he saw me sitting on the floor with a mallet in my hand driving the last of the tent pegs in. He and I had already become great friends but maybe this showed him I had even more initiative than he'd suspected. He soon asked me to be treasurer and I said yes and thoroughly enjoyed it as it gave me responsibility and got me out meeting people who were like-minded. Ever since then the Woodcraft Folk has been a major factor in my life.

I am a leader for the Elfin, Pioneer and Venture groups which cover three different age ranges. I am now also the chairman for the area network which covers a geographical stretch from Banbury to the Forest of Dean and takes in Oxford, Swindon and Gloucester and I am a trustee and vice-chairperson of the national organisation.

I go to meetings two evenings a week and help organise camps three or four times a year. I manage with a trailer tent which means the base of the bed is at wheelchair height and it has a toilet cubicle in there as well. A friend called Chrisman, a character in himself, puts it up for me but provided the camp is on a flat piece of ground, I can shuffle from my wheelchair to the bed so I can manage going to bed and to the toilet by myself.

In Woodcraft camp we do everything co-operatively. Camp is divided into clans and each clan has a job to do. One day a clan might be doing the cooking, the next site services which is dealing with the rubbish and recycling, the next they might be on toilets. We have someone responsible for the kitchen, another for activities, another for collecting wood, building the fire and looking after it. It works really well.

I have been a camp chief for five years. I think the reason they chose me is because I've got a big mouth and a loud voice and I can shout a lot so the kids tend to respect me. I can do very little of the practical things like putting tents up or seeing to the fire but I'm fairly good at keeping an eye on things and telling people what to do. If there are any problems or conflicts, I sort them out and make sure everything runs smoothly.

Over four days camping, people can get tired and bitchy and I try to mediate. We have a strict policy on drugs and alcohol which I enforce and I make sure hygiene standards are kept to in the kitchen and that everybody does what they are supposed to do.

I've also been a "KP" – kitchen provider – which involves working in a big mess tent for a whole week. The last one I did was a big international camp where there were 300 people in our "village" and I was responsible for feeding them for seven days. I got *so* tired. I was up at 7 a.m. to prepare breakfast for 8 a.m. and I didn't finish working until 10 p.m. I had to write the menus and shopping lists, make sure all the food arrived, fetch extra supplies if we ran out, supervise the cooks washing their hands and tying their hair back and make sure everything was cleaned up properly at the end of the day. Exhausting, but very satisfying.

Even if it pours, I can usually get across a field in my electric wheelchair. When it's wet we all gather in the communal marquee and I limit my drink so I don't have to head into the mud to go to the loo too much. Though it's pretty tough, my wheelchair has broken down twice, once when I was camp chief and the crossbar broke in half. I rang the wheelchair services and told them I was stuck in the middle of a field three miles outside Cheltenham but they said they couldn't do anything for three days. They hadn't got anyone they could call out. I said, "I bet you have," but they were adamant.

One of our leaders was a reporter and she had friends whom she phoned and told them the story and before you knew it we had the local TV station, the *Gloucestershire Echo*, the *Western Daily Press* and assorted photographers all tramping across this field to see me marooned with my broken wheelchair. And, do you know what? I got a replacement wheelchair the very next day. .

Involvement with the Woodcraft Folk did three very important things for me. First of all it gave me my confidence back after it had been completely destroyed. I am naturally a very determined, even bolshy, person but the period when I was breaking up with John had turned me into someone who, if you went "boo" to, I would jump. I was scared to say anything out of turn, particularly with John. Meeting Duncan and taking on responsibility at Woodcraft brought me out of myself again.

Secondly, it improved my social life by miles and gave me wonderful, long-term friendships. I was out of the house, in good company, active, busy and doing things with the children. It was perfect. And lastly – and most importantly – it gave me my determination back, it gave me that edge. It started me off fighting not only for what I want but for proper equality for all disabled people which now forms a big part of my life.

I had been treasurer for about three months when Woodcraft held a new leaders' training weekend. Unfortunately it was in a building which was impossible for me to get into. They said, never mind, don't worry about it, but all the other leaders were going and I really objected to being left out. I thought, blow this. I'm not standing for this, and I blew my top but it didn't make any difference.

So I decided to turn up anyway and sit outside in a silent protest. And that's what I did. I was there half an hour before the start of the session when Duncan and a couple of others were getting the place set up. Duncan said, "What are you sat there for?" and I said, "I've come for new leaders' training. It should be accessible. You say you are for equal opportunities and you are not."

Duncan thought I would sit there for half an hour and get bored but I stayed for an hour and a half as all the people came in, then I went home for something to eat and timed my return for when the meeting finished. I was sitting outside again as they came out. The next morning I was there again as people arrived and when they left and the same the third day.

Duncan got really embarrassed. He said, "You can't do this," and I said, "Why not?" He said, "It's wrong. It's bad," and I said, "No, it's making a point. This place should be accessible to everyone and that includes me." By the end of that weekend my point was well and truly understood. I got Woodcraft to accept that, if it promoted equality, that had to mean equal opportunities for disabled people to take part in their activities. So they moved to a new meeting place which was totally accessible with a disabled toilet and everything and that was great.

But that wasn't the end of my campaigning. About seven years ago Duncan and I decided to go to the annual general meeting which was being held at Loughborough Co-operative Society College. We arrived a bit late and registered and it never crossed my mind that access would be a problem. So I headed towards the hall and … stairs. The meeting was in a kind of theatre and there were about seven steep stairs. I looked at Duncan, Duncan looked at me and we thought, bloody typical!

Friends hauled me up the stairs which was very undignified and I was really annoyed because once I was up there I was reliant on people to get me down to go to the loo, plus there were more stairs to get to the microphone so I couldn't reach it. I asked Duncan to make a speech for me. He was embarrassed and didn't want to do it but to my mind to say your organization is all about equality for all and yet to have a meeting in a place that is non-accessible is totally unacceptable.

Duncan went to the microphone and said, "I don't usually do speeches but my colleague up there, Louise, is stuck. We say we are welcoming to all and I am really embarrassed about this, but we are not." He put forward a motion that in future the meetings should be accessible which was met with a standing ovation with everyone turning towards me, so then it was my turn to be embarrassed.

After that I was determined to improve things nationally so I started phoning the districts individually. People said it was not national policy to be accessible, or that they hadn't got anyone disabled anyway. I said, "Don't you think the reason why people don't come is because they are not going to embarrass themselves, unless they are as stubborn and determined as I am, to turn up to a group night when they can't get in, especially if they are children?"

I wasn't making much progress so in 2007 I plucked up enough courage to put my name forward to go on the council.

I wanted accessibility to be a national policy and I was fed up with being a lone voice. I put forward the motion that all weeknight activities should be accessible and that branches should have a sticker to advertise that they can cater for the deaf, visually impaired and wheelchair users. It got passed and I was voted on to the council for two years at the same time.

So now I have produced a form which branches can fill in about whether they have ramps, disabled toilets, etc., and I have designed a symbol based on an Australian logo. If the premises are totally accessible, the symbol is a person pushing themselves in a wheelchair which has the Woodcraft logo in the wheel, and if you need assistance to get in the symbol has someone standing behind the wheelchair. I did another one for places that are not accessible with a great big red cross over the wheel but it was suggested that nobody would want to advertise they are not open to disabled people so it was pointless.

I also joined the council's recruitment committee. I have got so much experience of recruiting carers and I know what to look for in hiring staff. I've been involved in appointing five of the 22 staff for the HQ in London. Ironically, that building is not accessible either so Woodcraft are moving to brand new offices. They said it would be very bad PR to ask the branches to put these stickers on saying they are accessible when the main office isn't. So I think I have achieved something.

In fact, things have improved a lot. When I first joined Woodcraft there were only three disabled members but at the last international camp I went to there were 3000 people – not even half the membership – and there were 12 in wheelchairs and about the same number on crutches.

I feel that I have achieved a lot through my leadership activities in the Woodcraft Folk, and I am proud of it. Around 300 kids have gone through my groups in Cheltenham in the 12 years I have been active and they have known me for what I am and I believe that as a result their attitudes towards anyone who is different because of disability or for any other reason will be more open throughout their lives.

The success of my first sit-in protest gave me the

confidence to take on the rest of Cheltenham. When the DDA – the Disability Discrimination Act – came in in 2004 I made and distributed posters to publicise the new regulations. At that time the only toyshop in Cheltenham was up an escalator and there was no lift or any other kind of access.

So I sat outside there and protested, pointing out to anyone who would listen that this flew in the face of equal opportunities for disabled people and now was breaking the new Disability Discrimination Act. I went right through town testing every shop I came to and, if I couldn't get in, I gave them a poster and a letter saying they had a month to make themselves accessible. And I said that, if you don't, I will take you to court.

The *Gloucestershire Echo* picked up the story and did a big report. When I returned to the shops a month later, 99% of them had complied with the law. That doesn't always mean building a ramp or putting in a lift – the law is that they have to make reasonable adjustments. So if the business is in a Regency building, for instance, as many in Cheltenham are, and subject to a preservation order, they only need to install a bell at street level and designate a member of staff to come down and find out what you want. I offer advice as well as threats and point out that the changes they have to make don't have to be expensive.

I did it not because I necessarily want to go into every shop in town but because it's not right that I should be denied the opportunity just because I use a wheelchair. Now other disabled people come to me if they come across a premises that is not accessible and I go along and point out their obligations under the DDA.

Sometimes people say they are renting. I don't care, they are offering a service and it should be for everybody so I tell them they have to speak to the landlord. Sometimes they blame council regulations so then I tackle the council. I've been told by council officials that compliance is not compulsory but I've got all the facts at my fingertips. I tell them that if the premises doesn't comply with the rules within a month, I will take it to court and also take the council to court for giving out the wrong information. I don't see myself as a disabled people's leader exactly, I'm just the one with the big mouth.

In truth, I feel the DDA doesn't go far enough and that disabled people are still treated as third-class citizens. I would be much happier if the UK was the same as America, which is a paradise for disabled people in comparison. There, all places have to be accessible and if they are not, they are simply closed down.

I also served for some years on the community health council which was an independent body which got patients' views on services before the trusts came in. I went to the hospitals to listen to old people who would complain about little things like paint peeling off the walls, and the children's hospital which was much more inspiring. I had to go to hospices as well which was sad. I found the patients knew they were dying and had accepted it; it was their loved ones who wanted them to live who were breaking their hearts. I watched them coming in, willing the person to live, putting a brave face on it and going away again in tears.

The job also covered mental disability and I had to visit an old Victorian mental institution. I still remember the cells, the smell, the coldness. I knew that disabled people had been incarcerated in such places in the past and I was only driving up the drive when I got this really eerie, panicky feeling, like I could hear screaming in my head.

I knocked on the door and was shown round and all the time I could feel the fear. I knew people had been scared in that place, the whole atmosphere was steeped in fear. It was a horrible feeling. I left there in tears and swore I would never go back. I can still feel the fear whenever I think about it.

In recent years I have started lecturing on disability in general and on the disabled and technology. I talk to students at Glasgow University about business ethics in the thalidomide case, where I give both sides of the story and leave it up to them to make a decision on whether on a business level they think what happened was ethical.

I also do ten lectures a year at a school in Cheltenham to Year 10. I talk about the history of disability, about my condition and how it occurred and how society's attitudes have transformed. I put it in the context of how children were treated in Romanian orphanages. The kids think, how ghastly, but it's the same as we were doing just a few decades ago. I talk about how disabled people used to be feared, pitied or put in freak shows, like the Elephant Man and Caterpillar Man, how religious leaders often said that having a disabled baby meant you must have done something wrong.

I tell them that their grandparents didn't use to see disabled people out and about and ask them how they would feel if they saw an alien that was pink with purple spots and green antennae. Most say they would be frightened and some say they would want to kill them. I tell them I have been married and had children and that I drive around – the boys in particular are interested in how I drive the car. I talk about how technology has transformed the lives of disabled people since the 1960s and how it can help in the future but that designers have to use common sense and to think realistically about how disabled people live their lives.

Often designers are far too fond of gadgets. They will invent some fancy arm to pick up the phone, for instance but I say, why should we want that? It's far more practical not to pick up the phone at all but to answer it by pressing a button. Simplicity is what you need, like when someone decided to attach a lawn mower motor to a wheelchair and, hey presto, invented the amazing electric wheelchair that now takes me pretty well anywhere I want to go.

I am very open with the kids. At each session I give them a challenge to come up with a question I am not prepared to answer and there hasn't been one. Just once a girl got close when she asked me, "Do you blame God for what you are?" I had to think about that for a bit but I said, "No, I blame man for what I am, not God. If there is a God."

Sitting on my mother's lap.

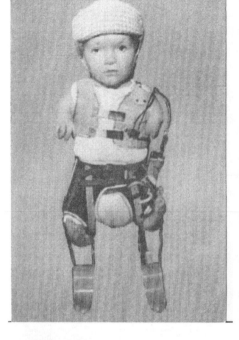

Aged two, wearing my first artificial limbs. I would fall over, hence the crash helmet.

My mother, father, sisters Claire and Lindsey, brother David and Luke the Labrador during the campaign for compensation for Thalidomide victims and their families in 1972.

Pop stars Cliff Richard and Olivia Newton John and footballer Mike England visited m family to support our campaign.

Cliff Richard gets down to my level.

Aged 14 with a friend's pet dog.

In 1973 I visited Lourdes with a church charity group. It was an inspirational trip.

I gave birth to my first child, Emma, on April 14, 1988.

Walking Emma and Jack (in the background) home from school in 1998.

Family portrait with John on Emma's first birthday.

Darren first proposed to me when we were 19 and I turned him down. But 27 years later we finally married in August 2008.

My daughter Emma and son Jack at the wedding.

On honeymoon in Las Vegas, August 2008.

Chapter Ten
Kidney Dramas

I STARTED HAVING SYMPTOMS of kidney trouble after I had Emma though I had no idea that was what it was at the time. My grandfather – my mother's father, Jack Whiteside – died of a heart attack and kidney failure after two years on dialysis but I had no idea it was hereditary. As I said before, who would have thought that nature could play such a cruel joke?

I got tired very easily and there were certain foods I couldn't eat, which tended to be anything healthy. I was fine on junk like crisps and burgers but if I tried to eat a salad I would be ill straight away. I also picked up infections very easily so it was like I was always off colour which is hard when you are trying to keep up with a toddler.

When I was pregnant with Jack I was in a lot of discomfort in my lower back. I went to hospital for my scan and was given the good news and the bad news – the baby was fine but I had polycystic kidneys. This meant there were multiple cysts both inside and on the outside of my kidneys which could only get worse and for which the only cure was to have dialysis first and then a kidney transplant.

They said it was a directly inherited condition which was a mystery at first as neither of my parents was ill but then I remembered my grandfather. I was advised to tell my mother to get checked out so I phoned my parents and they refused to believe me at first. She had been feeling tired but she had just put it down to advancing age.

It was a couple of months before she got checked out and

discovered she had an advanced stage of polycystic kidneys. Within a year she was put on a dialysis machine and then was lucky enough to be offered a kidney transplant, though that wasn't the end of the story. The first transplant failed because she was allergic to one of the anti-rejection drugs but another kidney was found for her and she recovered well.

As my pregnancy advanced I was often in dreadful pain either from an infection or when a cyst swelled and burst. I had made a solemn vow never to take any pills while I was pregnant and I'd learned to get past even the most intense pain by going to sleep but towards the end it got so bad I thought it was either me or him.

After Jack was born I felt better for a while but then a whole lot of problems seemed to pile up at once. My relationship with John was going downhill, he was messing around and we had our confrontation and I threw him out, after which I felt really down. For years he had been telling me I was fat and I was ugly, that I wasn't being a proper mum and didn't know how to control the kids. I had his mum telling me I didn't know how to run the house and I had the carers trying to take over Emma and Jack while I was trying to be as much of a mother to them as I could.

So I had lots of negatives around me at the same time as my kidney problems were getting worse and I often felt totally exhausted. I wasn't eating properly but I was drinking gallons. My face had gone a pasty grey colour, I slept for 10 hours a night and napped again during the day. I went for a check-up every six months and when Jack was a toddler the doctor warned me that I would probably soon have to go on dialysis. There was one big problem with that, however, which is that without arms and legs, I have no main veins where they could attach a tube. There is a procedure called PKD in which they fill a space in your abdomen with dialysing fluid and drain it off four times a day but they decided it wasn't practical for me so the upshot was that they put me on the emergency list for a kidney transplant.

Soon after that my results began to get a lot worse really quickly. I was being sick after every meal, drinking like a fish and sleeping most of the day. I was told that if no suitable kidney came up for me within four months they would have to put me on the PKD procedure.

I knew I couldn't rely on John to take over the children full-time when I went into hospital but I had to be ready to go immediately a kidney became available and fortunately Duncan promised to step in. As soon as I got the call I was to phone him and he would ring round a chain of people who would all help out.

On 20th May, 2001 I was driving the children to school – I used to leave the house at 7.30, drive to Emma's school, then to Jack's and get back at 9.15 – and was just leaving Emma's school when my mobile rang. It was the hospital in Oxford saying, "Can you be here in the next four hours?"

I started panicking. It's one thing to know you need a transplant and long for the day when a suitable kidney will be offered, but quite another suddenly to be faced with the prospect of having a life-threatening operation that very day.

I dropped Jack off at school though he was really crying and not wanting to let me go. He was frightened – I was frightened too but he felt it the most. I phoned Duncan and told him, "I've got a kidney!" and he promised to pick Jack up from school and take him to his house for his tea.

Then I phoned Emma's school to ask them to keep her there as it had boarding facilities, packed an overnight bag and set off to drive to Oxford though I found myself driving back towards Emma's school as I was on a kind of automatic pilot. Halfway there I came to, turned round and eventually got to the hospital where I had to ring the ward to ask them to send someone to help me get out of the car.

As I was waiting in the car park, feeling very alone and scared, my friend Chrisman turned up out of the blue. I said, "What are you doing here?" and he said, "You didn't want to be on your own, did you?" I was so touched I burst into buckets of tears.

They took some blood to do a tissue-type test at 10 a.m. and told me not to eat or drink anything which was hard as I was absolutely starving. Chrisman went really pale when a nurse asked him if he was a living donor! At 2 p.m. they came back and said the kidney was not a perfect match but it would do and I was going to theatre at 4 p.m. That brought on more tears of terror.

Then they came and told me I had to take these tablets, cyclosporine. I needed a really large dose – 1,500mg to knock out my immune system so the new kidney would not be rejected and they were massive things. I said I had a phobia about pills and they said I had better get used to them because I would have to take them for rest of my life. Between my fear and my phobia it took me three goes before I could keep them down.

Chrisman stayed with me the whole day until I was wheeled into theatre at 4 p.m. and was still there when I woke up. The surgeons had decided not to remove my old kidneys straight away to give the transplant time to get going and had managed to find a space in my abdomen just above my left leg to put in the new one. My dad was at my bedside when I first woke which I just about took in before I fell asleep again. When I woke for the second time I suddenly felt flooded with more energy than I'd had for a very long time and could finally tuck into a decent meal.

Jack came in the next day with Duncan who, as soon as he saw me, said, "Wow! You look like you've been on holiday." Though I was pretty sore all over, I felt well, all the colour had come back into my face, I was bouncing around, talking away and playing cards. My appetite returned, I began drinking normally and I was out of hospital in ten days.

So far as I know, I am the only four-limbs deficient Thalidomider to have a kidney transplant, at least in the UK, and everyone was delighted with the success of the operation. Unfortunately, I didn't feel that good for long as problems soon began with my old kidneys where the cysts were still growing so I continued to get episodes of excruciating pain and infections. That Christmas I was ill and by December 28th I was really bad with a rocketing temperature.

I spent New Year's Eve in hospital being sick while Jack and Emma went to stay at Duncan's. I came home a week later but after another few days a really big cyst burst and it was terribly painful. I got an infection and I was shivering so they took me back to hospital as an emergency and decided the kidneys had to come out.

You might have thought that I couldn't wait to get rid of them as they were the size of rugby balls, you could see them poking out of my back and I couldn't lie down comfortably. But the truth was that I didn't want them out because my mum had hers out six months before and it had nearly killed her.

I really didn't think I was going to make it through the operation so I decided I would have to put my affairs in order. I made my will and also contacted a solicitor to pursue my divorce. By then John and I had been living apart for eight years. I had petitioned for divorce initially on the grounds of his adultery but after we separated I hadn't proceeded with it.

Now I thought that if I died, everything I had would go to John and I was afraid that he might spend it all and there would be nothing left for the children. I knew the transplant could last many years, or only a few, it depended on the kidney. The reality was then, and still is, that I haven't necessarily got as long to live as the average person so I've got to be ready.

I finally got divorced in November, 2002. When I got the actual decree nisi it was like the end of an era, like a loss. Even though I hadn't been living with John for a long time, the reality of it doesn't fully hit you until you hold that piece of paper in your hand. From then on the only things we had in common were the kids and the fact that I kept his name.

I arranged with Duncan that he would be the children's guardian because I didn't feel John was reliable enough and I went into the operating theatre gripped with fear that I would never see them again. As it happened, my premonition very nearly came true – or actually did come true for a brief period when my heart stopped on the operating table and had to be restarted with an electric shock, ER style.

The operation was a lot more complicated than the surgeons had been expecting because it turned out my kidneys had somehow fused on to all my other organs, heart, liver, stomach and the new transplanted kidney, and they had to be delicately detached, one by one. They had started at 6 p.m., expecting to finish by 9 p.m. but didn't get through until three in the morning. Then they faced even more problems when they tried to stitch me up because the wound wouldn't stop bleeding, so they applied a kind of foam as a medical sealant. When I woke up the first thing I saw was this strange white foam all down my front which I thought must be coming from inside me.

My dad was there, I heard him saying, "she's waking", before I passed out again. The next time I came to I was a bit more with it and understood that I was in intensive care and that I'd been unconscious for four days. The kids were told nothing about how close I came to never seeing them again, just that I was asleep.

Finally, I began to recover but it was a very slow process which was to keep me in hospital for 11 weeks. Duncan and Chrisman and my friends from Woodcraft Folk came to see me every single day. They would bring Jack every other day and Emma at weekends. They were shocked at how I looked at first. I was full of tubes and was held together by metal staples all the way down my chest. I looked like Frankenstein and felt extremely weak. I was still taking the massive tablets to stop the new kidney being rejected and it would take me all day to get them down.

I had a reaction against the anaesthetic which upset my stomach. I was on a water bed which would vibrate every so often to try to prevent pressure sores. I couldn't sleep for the noise, I hurt all over, I was in a really bad way and feeling so sorry for myself I almost didn't want to live. After about seven weeks I was taken off the vibrating bed but I was still so weak with my muscles so wasted that I couldn't even lift a plastic spoon to feed myself. For a while all I ate was yoghourt but as I gradually managed to get more food inside me my strength began to return.

Meanwhile things were falling apart at home without me. The carer who was looking after the children with the help of Duncan and a limited amount of input from John suddenly announced she wanted to leave. I begged her to stay on for a month until I came out of hospital and could sort out a replacement and she initially agreed but then phoned again a week before my release date and said she was off there and then.

I had fluid on my legs from lying down for so long and couldn't even fit into my wheelchair. Anyway, I couldn't move off the bed to try to fit into it as I still had stitches in and was extremely sore. But nothing washed with her. She said, "The kids are at Duncan's, the dogs are in the house. I've packed and I'm going."

I was stuck helplessly in hospital, worried sick about the kids and furious with her for being so utterly selfish. OK, she had stayed on two weeks longer than she wanted but I couldn't understand how anybody could do that in the circumstances I was in, just abandon the kids and disappear. Once I'd calmed down a bit I began to think more clearly about what to do. I thought the quicker I got home the better but the hospital wouldn't let me out unless I had a nurse so I rang the nursing agency who agreed to send someone along the following Monday.

This was Friday and the children were supposed to be with their father for the weekend. Duncan had been wonderful but he had a wife and three children of his own so couldn't have mine all the time. And anyway, he thought they were John's responsibility so he had got hold of him and told him he had to look after them. So John had been at the house that week looking after Jack and the dogs but when Emma came home from her boarding school on the Friday night he'd had the cheek to take them both back to Duncan's and say, "I want to go out for the weekend, you take the kids." Duncan was stunned and said, "You are their father!" but John said, "Yes, but I've got plans and I'm going."

I was really embarrassed when Duncan and his wife came to see me on the Sunday and described the row they'd had with John. They said they had found him and the children on their doorstep when they had got home from work on the Friday and John had just given them their bags and left. Duncan's wife had tried to make him face up to his obligations but she said he was in such a mood, he would have just gone anyway.

On the Monday morning the doctor said he wanted me to stay in hospital for another two weeks but I felt I had absolutely no choice. The nurse wouldn't come if I was not at home, I had no nanny, my wonderful cleaner, Sue, couldn't look after the kids on her own, it was too much for Duncan to carry on caring for my children full time and John didn't care.

I just about managed to squeeze myself into my wheelchair after taking loads of water tablets and travelled home by ambulance but I was still in a lot of pain. Every single bump I went over in the road, I felt. I could barely move and it took me hours to do the simplest thing. The nurse turned up, then two hours later Jack arrived then Emma came home and we were all together again. The nurse stayed two weeks by which time I was able to get on and off the loo without help and just managed to shower using the shower board though I was still very tender.

John came round occasionally and my knight in shining armour, Duncan, popped in every two or three days. I wasn't able to drive after such a major operation but after a while I was able to get on a bus in my wheelchair so gradually started regaining my mobility and life returned to normal.

One unexpected by-product of my being so seriously ill was that one day my mother physically cared for me for the very first time since my brother, David, had hurt my foot when I was seven years old. It was during the period that I was eating nothing but yoghourt and she sat by my bed and said, "You've got to eat," then actually fed me.

And it turned out I was so glad she hadn't done it before because she was unbelievably bad at it. Taking just a small mouthful at a time was hard for me because I didn't feel like food and my mouth was full of ulcers but she went at it like a conveyor belt. The spoon went in the yoghourt pot then in my mouth, pot, mouth, pot, mouth, allowing me not a moment to swallow in between. It was awful.

Chapter Eleven
Trying To Help

Dr Claus Newman, head of the 'Leon Gillis Unit' at Queen Mary's Hospital in Roehampton, South-west London, where many thalidomide children were fitted with artificial limbs and helped towards independence.

THERE HAD NEVER BEEN a problem like thalidomide before so there was no established pattern in the health service in how to respond and things happened on an ad hoc basis. At Roehampton Hospital in South-west London, the Department of Health provided some money in 1964 to pay for one room, a nursing sister and an auxiliary to try to help the babies born as a result of the thalidomide epidemic of 1959-62.

By great good fortune the nursing sister was a remarkable woman called Gwen Mears who was very much ahead of her time. She was available because she had just resigned from her job in a unit looking after children with cerebral palsy when her insistence that a paediatrician should be appointed had been refused. An earlier job at a children's hospital had also come to an abrupt end when she confronted a neurosurgeon who was carrying out what was then experimental surgery in an attempt to relieve progressive water on the brain in children with spina bifida.

What usually happened was that the matron who accompanied the great man on his rounds ordered curtains to be drawn round the cubicles housing children who had had unsuccessful operations to spare him the sight and sound of these unfortunates. One morning Gwen was on duty when he visited and barred his way as he was about to walk past the first curtained cubicle. "No, Mr M****," she said, "*this* is your first patient." While the matron was pleased to see the back of her, she nevertheless recommended Gwen when the Unit at Roehampton was established.

Roehampton started as a military hospital during the First World War initially only for officers who had lost limbs. The development of artificial limb design and expertise in limb fitting gained the hospital a wide reputation for excellence and by 1964 the Department of Health decided that it might be a good place for children born without limbs. There were also new units established in Edinburgh and Oxford as well as at Chailey Heritage.

At Roehampton, a paediatrician already had an outpatient clinic there but he was not particularly interested in children with severe physical handicap, nothing unusual at the time. When I asked him if he might wish to play a role in the care of these unique thalidomide children with me after my appointment, he replied, "No thank you, my boy. They are all perfectly healthy, aren't they?"

Gwen was given her room and put in charge of liaising between the children, their families and the orthopaedic and limb-fitting surgeons at Roehampton. In about 1967 the Variety Club of Great Britain donated money for the building of a school room which was jointly used for nursing procedures for children with spina bifida and a place for the beginnings of highly specialised primary education.

In a role she continued until her retirement, Gwen listened to the parents, gently asked questions, familiarised herself with what was going on in their and their children's lives, and then used her wide nursing experience to help. She gave advice on things like how best to secure a nappy on a baby lacking legs or how to help such an infant to sit up. She also listened and counselled parents facing distress and family break-up, which sadly happened to many couples because of the strain. In the early years, she got support only from the orthopaedic surgeon,

Sir Leon Gillis, after whom the Unit was named, and a few social workers.

Also in the early 60s, Lady Mary Hoare, wife of the then Lord Mayor of London, established a trust to help the Thalidomiders. She was ahead of her time in that she was convinced that children cared for in their own homes would have a better chance of happiness and of personality development than they would living in residential centres. She established a corps of Lady Hoare Social Workers who visited families and helped to assess their needs. This work continues even today, transformed into the Thalidomide Society which provides information and support. I got to know several of these social workers and they provided an interesting reflection of contemporary social ideas. Their attitudes ranged from an almost feudal outlook, expecting a harassed mother to welcome them with an invitation to sit down and have a cup of tea, to a modern one of rolling up their sleeves, helping with whatever was necessary and getting hold of practical aids such as a washing machine. Providing a real service was fundamental in developing trust between the social workers and the Roehampton Unit staff, and the parents and children.

I had once come across a thalidomide baby with extremely short arms and legs in 1962 when I was working as a paediatric registrar at the Whittington Hospital in North London. But the child did not survive and the cause of the condition was at that time unknown, so I knew little about the condition. In 1969 I was appointed consultant paediatrician to the Westminster Hospital to look after infants and children with congenital heart conditions. At that time the Department of Health had stipulated that all consultants must do at least nine NHS sessions, and this accounted for two, so my future colleagues arranged additional sessions in a number of other hospitals, a patchwork which included two sessions at the "Children's Prosthetic Unit" in Roehampton, in other words, the thalidomide unit. No preparation or training for the care of these children was thought necessary, perhaps because interest in child development as distinct from diseases of children was at that time in its early phase in the UK.

So I became director of the Roehampton Unit in 1969, landed with the seemingly impossible job of helping these children lead normal lives, and I had to work out the best strategy. From my pre-interview research, I had learned that a carefully planned unit for thalidomide children in Liverpool had failed before treating a single patient because of disagreements between a number of newly appointed staff members and the place had become a store for mattresses. I was determined not to repeat their mistake: if I was going to make a snowman, I was going to start with a small nucleus and roll it to accumulate layer upon layer until I had got a critical mass which I was able to mould into a solid form. I wasn't going to put all the "snow" together in a big heap and hope it would stand up. Despite my lack of training with limbless children, the challenge suited me as I was always fascinated by every area of medicine. My patchwork of sessions meant I was working in paediatric cardiology, looking after newborn infants, working on a general children's ward and with children in two otherwise adult units, and the thalidomide children. It was fabulous as I faced any number of challenges every day.

I built up the Unit to include a registrar, a houseman, Gwen the nursing sister and her staff, occupational therapists, physiotherapists, a social worker, clinical and educational psychologists and a child psychiatrist, plus we had a close liaison with orthopaedic and limb-fitting surgeons and also plastic surgeons. It was truly a "snowman" of many skills. Since many of these professionals used only a small number of sessions for work in the Unit, it was a highly economical arrangement. Little did I know that this very economy would be part of its ultimate downfall.

Our Unit worked in a very unusual way by the standards of the medical profession at the time because everyone was regarded as an equal member of the team. Anybody suitable who knew the children and their progress could chair the regular weekly meetings called at the time of the child's admission. We would identify exactly what the purpose of the admission was, decide what approach we would take and draw up a timetable for treatments and training. In the week after discharge we met again to review what, if any, progress had been achieved, then recommendations were distributed to consultants involved with the child, his or her doctor, the community paediatrician, the social worker and sometimes teachers as well.

Our multi-disciplinary team worked harmoniously and creatively. We employed a dancer who taught limbless children to dance which they did with an enthusiasm which proved their imagination was undamaged. The local education authority seconded to us two teachers whose work was invaluable because they were fascinated by the problems of integrating severely handicapped children into mainstream school. What we learned from their input was that the academic achievements of the thalidomide children were far below what they should have been. Their intelligence was the normal spectrum so some of them were fabulously able but teachers generally believed that if you don't have arms you can't possibly complete any tasks. If the children did manage the tasks, they were often overwhelmed with admiration, so they were rarely intellectually stretched. Our teachers acted as advocates for the children to get over this and when the children transferred to secondary school, writing speed became a problem so alternative ways of keeping notes and writing answers had to be found.

I did two sessions a week in the Unit being presented with the challenge of helping children who could not enjoy doing what other children of the same age could do. Since I knew nothing about it I spent the first year watching and talking to the limb-fitting surgeons and technicians, fascinated by what they could do. The limb fitter at Roehampton, Iain Fletcher, was an absolute genius at adapting any sort of wood or leather to any human shape at all.

When a child was referred to the unit they were first interviewed by Gwen to discuss their main problems. Then they would be seen by the occupational therapist, a social worker, myself and anyone else relevant. The occupational therapist would study how they coped at home, travelling or at school and whether they could benefit from any of the available aids. These might simply be a dressing stick and a loop sewn into their pants to fit the stick into or maybe a device fixed to the wall which they could use to clean themselves, or a shower adaptation.

The purpose was to try to fit the home, the clothing and the routines to the child's particular anatomy and preferred way of doing things and to make the adaptation applicable to as many situations inside and outside the home as possible. For example, if someone had no arms so couldn't easily get coins out of a purse, they might have a season ticket sewn into their clothes.

Often the parents helped to design what was needed. The father of one child worked in a garage where he used a pneumatic jack. He adapted the technology of the jack to develop a wheelchair seat which could be pneumatically raised or lowered to a variable height for a child to reach a table, for instance. Plus he invented a platform fixed to the side of the bath with a button which his son could touch to be raised to the right height so he could slide across to another platform inside the bath. All the different ideas and inventions would be individually tailored to the child's needs, the child would be taught how to use them and after a few weeks we would review how things had gone.

If something new was needed or repairs had to be done, the technician might mock it up first in cardboard then make it out of metal in our own workshop. The most useful invention of all was the variable height wheelchair and the most dramatic was a rather Heath Robinson chin-operated feeding device. The child put his chin into a raised cup and, by pressing down, operated a lever and system to which a fork or spoon was attached. It made the fork go into a plate of food and then, by a system of pulleys and wheels, got the food to the child's mouth. It sounds like a punishment, but it worked quite well. The majority of the children were able to eat at table, even those with very short upper limbs. By leaning forward and sideways they were just able to reach the plate and bring the spoon up. They usually had enough fingers to hold a spoon and we often lengthened the handle or put a metal loop on the end of it.

The workshop also made a spoon with a cutting edge to cut down on the amount of cutlery they had to handle. That came out of thinking laterally about what a knife, a spoon or a fork were actually for and realising that the same functions could be achieved differently. Eventually they all devised their own comfortable ways of eating but it was also important to discuss with their parents about what they would find acceptable if they wanted to take the child out to eat in public. This was the end of the 50s and beginning of the 60s when few disabled people were seen out and about and people were more sensitive. These days you see people of all sorts of shapes and sizes and colours and being different from the norm is no longer a big deal.

In hindsight, we perhaps attached too much importance in those days to the idea of the need for independence at almost any price. The help of an assistant or friend to do things obviously increases a disabled person's dependence on others but it results in a more normal life because it means spending less effort and time on activities normally taken for granted.

We encouraged the thalidomide children to use their feet in the Unit, even though it was thought to delay their learning how to use their artificial upper limbs. Not every child could use their feet expertly but some became highly expert. Unhappily, now, 50 years later, the subtle joints, tendons and muscles necessary are changing and increasing pain and stiffness is restricting such function.

After a while I realised that the limb fitters were having very considerable success helping children with a partial lack of lower limbs but, sadly, everything else they came up with turned out to be actually detrimental to the children. The arms we made, in particular, were not very good. The children became immobile when they were wearing them and were not able to play like they normally did. I watched children falling over and not being able to get up again without someone to help them because of the weight of the arms and also because they created big problems with balance. The early versions of the metal harness round the chest to which the arms were attached was almost like a suit of armour. It had quite wide shoulders with these mechanical limbs hanging from them with metal hands on the ends. The children also had to carry gas cylinders on their backs to power them.

They worked the arms by pressing switches or manipulating a system of pulleys inside the shoulders with their hands or by moving their own shoulders. For instance, if a child moved his shoulder forward, it would make the arm go up. We taught them to reach out and grasp things but the disadvantages far outweighed the advantages. Indeed, the only arm I saw that worked was for someone who only had forearm loss below the elbow. In that case electrodes were attached which the child was able to activate by moving muscles to make the false hand move. Eating at table was the only time when the arms were useful as the children were able to use an upper limb prosthesis to feed themselves to some extent and we felt it was more acceptable that they could sit at the table and eat with other people rather than having to be fed. But in general an arm is too complex to make artificially with any success: just to stretch out your arm, pick something up and bring it to your mouth is actually a very complicated procedure.

When I saw that however hard the limb makers tried to make them lighter, however much work they did – and they did an enormous amount of work, all tribute to them – the children were hindered by these arms and harnesses and better off without them, I had to speak out. Unfortunately, Iain Fletcher, who had put so much into creating them, took deep offence and left the Unit.

Despite our successes, as time went on the Unit faced serious challenges. At that time the success of treatments for disabled people was measured in "quals", that is the quality of life. I was hoping we could raise a Thalidomider's "qual" from maybe 20 to 25 but nobody could find we actually made this difference.

In the first place the occupational therapists were not keen to observe the technique, but even when they did we were not able to define any objective benefit from what we were doing.

The sort of thing that would happen is that the children would act like performing monkeys when they were in the Unit and use the aids we invented for them to pick things up but then would throw them away as soon as they got home. So it was very hard to measure something that would justify our activities, plus the occupational therapy team knew their patients intimately and the attempt to quantify this knowledge in an artificial way was unpopular and was resisted.

After a while I decided to go with the tide and stopped the measuring process because it was psychologically very damaging to the team. I believed that the independence training we provided for the children was our best and there appeared to be no one else who could improve on the Unit's performance. It was crucial for the growing thalidomide children and young people that there was a Unit for them with confident therapists and staff and to destabilise it by insisting on a new pattern of attempted measurement of what we were achieving would be destructive. Later I came to believe that the actual physical help we gave the children was a lot less important to them than the psychological impact. Speaking to the young people when they were older I realised that, even if they never used our ingenious devices, they would have been devastated if nobody had tried to help them.

If you have something wrong with you that you are afraid of, for instance a congenital heart defect, you will be desperate to find a specialist who knows all there is to be known about the latest ideas and treatments. Even if he or she cannot do anything for you, just talking to an expert helps enormously. It was the same for our patients and their families – they needed to know they were being offered the best that human ingenuity could come up with.

Some of the Thalidomiders believe that our efforts were primarily aimed, not at helping them do what they wanted, but to make them look "normal" and therefore more acceptable to the wider society. My opinion is that our ideas of what we should do and our motivation evolved over time.

Initially we thought in terms simply of replacing something they had lost. If you've lost a leg, we will make you an artificial leg, you've lost an arm, so here's a new arm. The concept of the function of the false limb was thought to be self-evident.

What we learned was that, with the leg, the function is obvious, but with the arm it is too complicated. Making artificial limbs began in wartime and if a soldier loses a leg it is perfectly obvious he needs to walk again although society didn't have the imagination to see that just to walk was only the beginning of a long struggle to get back to normality.

When it became clear that there was not very much use for upper limb equipment, the arms became in practice for show. This was far from being unimportant, particularly when the children were going through adolescence. Then we made them "dress" arms which could be used to hold a glass, which was all that was needed at a party.

As we realised that function was the key we started to analyse each situation the children were likely to confront and to determine what was necessary for them to function as best they could in that situation. For instance, in the house there could be a series of switches that someone without arms can reach, one each for opening the door, putting on the radio, opening the curtains, boiling the kettle, closing the windows, and so on. A system for controlling the person's whole environment was developed which was infinitely better than them being weighed down by a set of unwieldy arms.

Even when we invented an aid that worked well, we still had to convince the people who cared for the children every day to use it. Generally, if we were able to prove to the parents that something was good, they would take it on but we often found that infant school teachers were harder to convince.

They were very frightened, quite understandably, of a child getting hurt while in their care. Most of them felt that someone with an upper limb deficiency shouldn't be allowed to take part in sport, for instance, as they could fall over and get injured. What we then did was to send an occupational therapist to the school while the sport was being played to advise on how to manage any dangers.

We found that issuing written advice was not enough. If a parent or teacher is terrified of a child doing something, having someone in an ivory tower tell you that your concerns are irrational is not going to be enough to reassure you. The only solution had to be practical and demonstrable. We learned not to promise anything unless we could do something that actually worked efficiently.

Of course, our job had as much to do with building relationships with the parents as it was trying to improve things for the children. Just as the children came from every section of society, so we had every variety of parent from the very rigid and intellectually limited to the highly intelligent and sophisticated and from the totally loving and accepting to those who could not bear the sight of their babies.

At a guess about 20% of the more seriously affected children were rejected by their parents to the extent that they were prevented from living at home. This accorded with established specialist advice at the time in that some mothers were wrongly told that their limbless child had been stillborn, were not shown their baby and so did not discover that their child was still alive until some weeks later. I kept a "Black Book" in which I entered the worst of such instances but professional opinion fortunately changed enough and in time to make it unnecessary for me to use it in an argument for better practice.

In general, the more severe the externally observable handicap, the more likely the child was to be rejected but there were many exceptions to this. Some badly affected children were kept at home and their parents and extended family made every effort to raise them while others were put straight into Chailey Heritage or an equivalent institution within weeks of birth and others were sent there as toddlers when the parents could not cope with taking them out into the world.

We met some very strange situations. I remember a mother and her eight-year-old child who arrived with one arm tightly bandaged against her chest. On unravelling the bandage, a wasted and now nearly useless but otherwise normally formed arm was revealed with just a thumb deformity on the hand. This was this parent's response to having had an "imperfect" child.

There were other most unhappy cases. Our knowledge of sexual abuse only developed in the late 1970s and I remember three girls who were in residential care in a rural area hinting to nursing staff about things we did not immediately believe or understand.

When the thalidomide children were assessed at 11 or 12 years old for legal compensation, it was found that many experienced severe and sometimes prolonged periods of psychological stress. Indeed, the prediction by psychiatrists was that a dire 30 to 40% would suffer psychological problems in later life, and maybe 100% of those who grew up at places like Chailey Heritage rather than at home.

Yet virtually all these predictions have proved to be wrong and in this, again, the Thalidomiders have taught the medical profession a good deal, since in the event the vast majority have achieved remarkable success in adapting to adult life. I think the reason the predictions were so inaccurate may be that the earlier psychiatrists were not able to distinguish between environmental stress and the inherited personality.

The truth seems to be that most of the children had the inherent psychological strength to overcome severe emotional stress as well as serious physical handicap which has shown us that the severity of a handicap does not necessarily correlate with the ability to adapt as an adult and to have a successful life. There aren't any genes for personality, so far as I know, but there has to be an inherited difference in the capability of coping in adversity.

I did, in fact, receive an early indication that a pessimistic outlook need not be correct when I was invited to dinner by Lady Hoare to meet an American preacher who was having a great deal of success with his charismatic church. There was an interesting discussion of different topics and it was not until well after he had finished the first course that I suddenly realised that he had no arms and had been smoothly eating his soup with his feet. He was enjoying a successful adult life despite the worst possible beginnings, born with severe physical handicap, rejected by his single mother, a childhood spent in a string of foster placements and residential care homes including episodes of abuse. Yet he had been able to rise above all this, without any professional input, because of his innate talents and strength of character.

Some Thalidomiders have made the charge that they were "experimented" on, implying that this was a bad thing. But we live in a technological society so we tried to come up with a technological solution to their predicament. The limb fitting service and the universities worked hard to invent many things and for the lower limbs they had considerable success even if wheelchair use became increasingly common as the Thalidomiders grew older. The results were much less successful for upper limb deficiency and the children often enough hated to be confined in their heavy harnesses with their gas-powered limbs hissing on sadly limited function. Yet even when such efforts proved unsuccessful, I strongly believe that there was a powerful and positive effect for the families. If we had not responded with our best efforts, everyone would now say that the Thalidomiders had been shamefully neglected and it would have been even more psychologically damaging for them to have felt totally ignored and forgotten which would have been a disaster.

In Germany there were about ten times as many Thalidomiders as in the UK. They chose a path similar to ours except that they were far more convinced they were doing the right thing so would brush aside objections from the parents with the "we know best" attitude with the result that more of their children were subjected to being made to wear artificial limbs which were detrimental.

In 1993, two years before I was due to retire, I was called to a meeting with the Department of Health and Social Security to discuss the way forward. Unfortunately, this coincided with one of the periodic squeezes on Health Service resources when chief executives could gain salary increases and other recognition if they achieved savings. Our C.E.O. at Roehampton had never visited the Unit, and once asked me why it took longer for us to deal with a child admission than it did in the Ear, Nose and Throat department to take out a pair of tonsils. The Ministry doctors said that our work was wonderful, we were wonderful, everything was wonderful, but they had no money for us.

Because our spending was below a million pounds per year, irrespective of what we did, we could not be accorded "Supraregional" status which would have protected us and our funding. So much for effective management.

The Unit was officially closed in 1995 when I retired and the rest of the staff were sent to work elsewhere. But we didn't want to stop so three loyal colleagues and I continued to provide out-patient clinics without the knowledge of the manager and chief executive for another five years, which was crazy. Then even that facility stopped.

Since the 1970s I had continued as medical adviser to the Thalidomide Trust, set up to administer the compensation funds that had been granted to the Thalidomiders. With the appointment of a new Director, the Trust developed a much more active interest in the changing life situations of the beneficiaries and we discovered a Unit with a philosophy like Roehampton's in Stockholm, Sweden. It was some time later that we learned that some Swedish visitors to our Unit in the 1980s had liked what they saw and developed their own unit on similar lines. The King is dead, long live the King!

I believe that the Ex Centre in Stockholm is now the only unit in Europe with specialised facilities for congenitally limb-deficient children and adults. But the Trust has not been idle. We are developing a service by experts in different disciplines, electronically interconnected, so that questions and requests from Thalidomiders can be answered or referred to people with greater knowledge. The aim is to use local N.H.S. facilities in the first instance but it is not always easy for someone with many different but connected problems, facing a GP whose practice manager watches to make sure that he or she does not exceed the usual seven minutes and only one problem or symptom per visit! When local resources have been exhausted and problems remain, Thalidomiders can be referred on to experts anywhere in the country who have previously agreed that they can be contacted for advice or treatment. There is also work in progress to develop a Europe-wide network for information and hopefully for expert treatment.

There is unhappily little doubt that the needs of the Thalidomiders are again increasing. As they head towards 50, their problems are mostly to do with degeneration: they are beginning to suffer from hip problems and arthritis, just like many people in the able-bodied population, problems that no one would have predicted 50 years ago that they would live long enough to suffer.

But projects are under way that will help to find answers. It may be premature to say that Cinderella has been at long last been invited to the Ball, but at least the tickets are being designed and printed.

Chapter Twelve
A Mother's Story

Margaret Hogg, mother of David

IF IT HAD BEEN left to doctors, I think most thalidomide babies would have been brought up in institutions like Louise because very few of them would have gone home from hospital with their mothers. If I had not come from a family which had learned to pull together during difficult times, that is what might have happened to David and me.

It was 1960, I was 18 and my husband, Bill, was in the RAF in Germany when I went into labour 11 days late. I had been very happily married for 15 months, I had had no problems with the pregnancy, not even any morning sickness, so I had no fears of anything going wrong. I went into Eastern General Hospital in Edinburgh where I proceeded to give birth to David without complications late on a Monday night. The first hint I got that anything was wrong was when they whipped him away immediately without me even seeing him. They just told he was "blue" and needed oxygen – that was the way doctors talked to patients in those days.

The next morning my mother and mother-in-law came to see me, then they went to see David. Afterwards they left the hospital without telling me anything so I was left fretting and worrying, imagining all kinds of horrors. Later that morning a doctor came and said a whole lot of long medical words at me which didn't mean a thing to me.

That just made things worse. I was in a terrible panic by

then. I wondered what on earth was going on, what strange creature had I produced? I had heard of Down's Syndrome and spina bifida but I reckoned it couldn't have been those because the doctor would have used those words and I would have recognised them. Despite all my worries, however, just one thought repeated itself loudly and continuously in my head, blotting out all others: "I want to see my baby!"

I annoyed the staff over and over again asking them to bring my baby to me until they were fed up with me so at 1.30 p.m. on the Tuesday afternoon they said that after my afternoon sleep they would bring him for his feed. They walked in with him wrapped tightly in a blanket with just his face showing, handed him to me, gave me a bottle to feed him with and left.

Alone in my hospital room, I finally got to meet my son who opened one eye to gaze at me. I started talking to him, whispering, "Why are you not opening your other eye?" I loosened the blanket and gently unwrapped him. As I looked him over, I thought his arms must have slipped out of the sleeves of his sleepsuit so I reached to push them back in, and that's when I realised he had no arms to speak of.

As I undressed him, I saw that he had just tiny sproutings from his shoulders with a hand on each and three fingers on each hand. I also saw that one leg was shorter than the other and that his right foot was turned in as a club foot. I can't remember exactly what I thought except that I was just left wondering what all that fuss had been about with all those long medical words. To me, he was my baby, and my heart went out to him.

I proceeded to wrap him up again and fed him. Then the nurse came back and asked me if I knew how to wind him which I did as I had already looked after other babies. So I burped him and she whisked him off again, still without saying a single word about what he was like. Soon afterwards a doctor came and said, in that patronising tone they used in those days, "I believe you have had baby and have had a look at him." I said, "If you had told me what was wrong this morning in words I could understand, I wouldn't have got upset at all.

He's my baby."

The doctor asked, "What do you intend to do with him?" I said, "What do you mean?" He said, "We have two or three options of homes you can send him to." I said, "No, there is only one option. He goes home with me." The doctor persisted, going on with his lofty attitude: "We have been discussing it. It is far better for him to go into a home." I said again, "There's only one home he is going into and that is *my* home. With me."

I have learned since that 95% of the mothers got that kind of reaction from doctors. It was not surprising that some gave into the pressure and sent their babies to be brought up in homes and others were separated from their babies long enough to damage the bonding process. Quite a few gave birth at home and had their babies whipped away to hospital when they had barely seen them so missed that vital first 12 to 14 hours. Some mothers were mortified that they had produced a disabled child and didn't know how to face it at first and the doctors' attitude made it a lot worse.

I was asked not to discuss "baby" with other mothers in the hospital in case it upset them and every time I fed him he was taken straight off to a little room by himself while I was also alone in a separate room. I have learned that a lot of the thalidomide babies didn't survive. We in the thalidomide community have our suspicions that, if they were poorly at birth, many were left without proper care until they died, but we can't prove it. I felt a fierce love for this vulnerable little thing, very protective, and the medical profession's attitude just reinforced my feelings.

Looking back, it seems amazing I was strong enough to resist the pressure when I was so young and my husband was abroad. But it was because I had grown up in a warm family who knew about how hard it was to lose people you love. My father was killed in World War II when I was two and a half. My mother remarried, I adored my second father but eight years later he was killed at work. I had to grow up very fast to look after my two younger sisters while my mother worked to keep us all.

My younger sister was six and the youngest was two and a half when my stepfather died and we grew used to joining forces and facing adversity as a team. My younger sister set the table for tea and helped me clean the house while the little one took on her share of chores as soon as she was old enough. My mother was always very proud of us and used to call us her "three smart girls".

Three or four days after David was born I asked the doctor with the long words why he hadn't opened his left eye. He told me he didn't have a left eye as it had never developed, and he didn't know how much sight he had in his right eye which has a streak across it, known as a "columbine".

I soon felt ready to go home. My mother had phoned the air force's family association who had got in touch with Bill and he had arrived on the Thursday. He came straight in and I had to ask the nurse to bring David to me. She marched in with him, plonked him on the bed and walked out without a word. I lifted him up and showed him to Bill who said, "Oh, I didn't understand what they were telling me before." It was hard because Bill was only home for a fortnight but he loved David just as much as I did from the beginning.

I was living with my mother and I had to go home from hospital leaving David behind as he was a little underweight which is perhaps hardly surprising as they were feeding him on Carnation condensed milk. I phoned up and went to see him every day, longing to take him home, but they kept saying, "He's not ready yet." Just about every time I went to the hospital either a doctor, a nurse or the hospital almoner (who was in charge of social care) said to me, "Let him go into a home. He will never lead to anything, he won't live past childhood." How wrong they were!

One day in November I went to visit and found him wrapped in a cotton blanket with a nappy and gown on waiting for an ambulance to transfer him to Leith hospital children's ward, though nobody had told me. They said; "Now you are here, you can take him in a taxi." I said I had no money for a taxi so they said they would pay.

Leith hospital was better though he was still only at his

birth weight when he finally came home three weeks later. I had taken a bag of baby clothes in with me every day ready to dress him and bring him home and one day as I was sitting beside David's bed with the bag on my knee, the doctor said, "You will need those today, you can take him home." That was when I broke down in tears, for the first time since David was born, because a doctor had been nice to me.

I said through my sniffles, "Are you not going to tell me to put him in a home too?" No matter how many times they said it to me, I never once even considered it. David was mine, and in my eyes he was a normal baby, minus two arms. He had a right to grow up at home and have a normal childhood.

There was no way I was going to hide him away either though sometimes the reaction of other people was hilarious. The day after I came home I got him dressed up and took him out proudly in his pram down to the shops. We lived in a small mining village outside Edinburgh where I had known everyone all my life so everyone I saw stopped to look at the new baby. One said, "Isn't he bonny?" I said, "What else do you expect? He's mine." She said, "I thought he only had one eye?" I said, "Yes, he only has one." She said, "No, he's got two eyes. I thought he only had one eye." I said, "What did you expect, that he had one eye in the middle of his forehead, like Cyclops?" That was the only upsetting reaction, everyone else was fine.

I had more problems with one of the health visitors. She came to my house to weigh David once a fortnight but in between I took him to the clinic where several friends who had babies at the same time were taking theirs. When the health visitor saw me she demanded, "What are you doing here?" I said, "I brought David to be weighed." She said, "Just bring him through to this other room, we will get him undressed in here." I said, "No, I will do it here with my friends."

She took hold of David and marched off with him to the other room. I chased after her and asked her why she was doing it there and she said it might upset the other mothers to see him. I said, "If that's your attitude, I won't be back," and stormed off with him. My mother rang the health visitor later and told her, "He's Margaret's baby. If she doesn't want to hide him away from the rest of the world, that's the way it's going to be." My G.P. came to the rescue. He said he would weigh David and give him his injections and I could wait in the waiting room in full view of all the other patients with his blessing.

When he started sitting up in his pram, David was an exceptionally beautiful child. He had thick blond curls any little girl would have envied. When he was nine months old we went to Butlin's holiday camp where he came second in a bonny baby contest. The judge said he would have come first if only he had opened his other eye – I didn't tell them he didn't have one.

He sat up at the normal age, crawled by shuffling along on his bottom and walked at a year old. We never made any accommodation for his disability. We never said he couldn't do anything. We said, "There's no such word as 'can't' in this house." I told him, "You *try* to do it." He was spoilt by his grandparents and aunts and uncles but not by us. He knew that throwing a tantrum would not get him anywhere but mostly he was a placid baby and toddler.

David has now got arms three inches long with a hand with three fingers on each. It's surprising what he can do with them as he is very strong and can lift heavier weights than I can. As a toddler he played with his cars with his feet or put them on a table or lay on the floor to play with them. He had a little stool in front of the sink and his cup was kept on the worktop so he could climb up and get himself a drink. Once a neighbour was round when he asked me to get him a drink and I told him to get it himself. She said, "Ooh, you are cruel." I said, "Not at all. He is going to have to do these things when I am not with him, so he has to learn."

Other children sometimes asked, "Why have you got little arms?" David would say, "Because I was born that way." David never asked us why he was like he was but I explained to him early on that something went wrong when he was in my tummy. I told him it didn't make any difference to us, he was my little boy and he was loved just the same as anyone else. It was just that he had to learn to do things more quickly or in a different way from other people.

He was always very open and friendly and he used to get out of the house and go wandering down to the local shops where he asked for sweets and told them that his mum would be coming along to pay for them later. The police brought him back a couple of times saying, "Does this little man belong to you?" Once when he was about four he said he was leaving home and going to stay with his granny. He had a little case which he had packed with all his toy cars and his pyjamas. I said I'd take him along there and when we arrived granny asked him why he wanted to live with her and he said, "My mum's not nice to me." It was because of something he had done so she told him that if he had done that in her house he would have had his bum smacked. He thought about it for a bit and then said, "Mum, I think I will come back to live with you."

He went to school at five and his first year was fantastic. He had a beautiful young teacher who was prepared to help him go to the toilet which he couldn't manage on his own then. But in his second year he had an old battle-axe who would not give him any help at all so he often came home soiled – there were no teachers' assistants in those days. I battled with the Education Department but in the end I had to give in and he was transferred to a special school for physically disabled children. It was a lovely school but they did a short day – 10 a.m. to 3 p.m. with an hour's sleep in the middle – so he didn't get a full education. He learned to read and write and do his sums and he painted beautifully, using a long brush.

He left school at 15 and went to Tile Hill College in Coventry, a residential place for the physically disabled where quite a few Thalidomiders went. He bunked up with Eddie Freeman and they had a ball. Eddie was four-limbs deficient but hadn't a care in the world. The two of them used to go down to the chip shop on Eddie's electric wheelchair with David riding on the back. Years later we met someone on holiday who came from that area and he vividly remembered the two boys careering down to the chip shop together like that.

David had the usual adolescent hiccups but nothing major. He never had a surly attitude and he didn't go through a self-conscious phase. He has got a wide variety of friends in every walk of life and frequently jaunts off with them on foreign holidays and has had several girlfriends. He eats using a knife and fork, leaning forward to reach the plate, and can look after himself so friends sometimes ask him why he still lives with his parents It's probably because life is so easy for him. This house has been adapted for him – we had an extension built on to give him his own space – and he comes and goes as he wants. I cook his meals and do his laundry, helped by carers who come in for six hours a week. They also take him shopping and make his meals when I am away.

His first job was working for the Scottish Spastic Society in Edinburgh answering the phone. When we moved to Barnsley 20 years ago, he went to work for the Dial-a-Ride scheme for disabled people but just got paid expenses. Most Thalidomiders had the same experience because when they were a lot younger, employers were not prepared to do the necessary adaptations in offices and shops which would have enabled them to work. Since the Disability Discrimination Act was passed a lot more Thalidomiders are finding employment, a few of them in social services on disability issues. But there are many who are not employed who should be.

After the Dial-a-Ride scheme came to an end, David hasn't had another job though he has tried many times to get one. Usually employers said they turned him down because of his eyesight – he is registered blind with 20% vision in one eye – but they never gave him an opportunity to show what he could do. He has done computer courses at college. He goes off to computer shows where he helps people with their computers. His knowledge of computers is massive. He uses no visual aids except a bigger font when printing. He can do anything on the computer and has such an easy-going attitude to life.

Everybody used to ask me what had happened to make David the way he was and I always said that I didn't know; it was just one of those things. The whole time I was expecting our second son, George, who was born in June, 1964, people asked if I wasn't frightened that it would happen again. I said no, God couldn't be so insensitive as to let it happen again.

I always believe everything happens for a purpose and that God doesn't give you anything that you cannot bear. I believe God doesn't do anything without thinking about it first. That was the way I was brought up. I think now He sent David to try me, and I have been tried. Before it came out that his condition was caused by thalidomide, I thought he was on this earth to prove that people who are not perfectly formed could still live a full and fulfilling life.

When the information about thalidomide first started coming out, I didn't connect it to David because I hadn't taken anything for morning sickness. But I joined the Thalidomide Society anyway because it was open to families with children with similar impairments. As he grew older and the compensation battle was getting to court, social workers started asking me, "Do you think it could be thalidomide?" I said I didn't think so as I had not had morning sickness but then someone told me that it wasn't only prescribed for morning sickness.

The only thing I had suffered from was bronchitis early on in my pregnancy for which my GP had prescribed a cough mixture. It was the only medication I took in the whole nine months. So I went looking for my medical records only to find they had disappeared which was quite a common problem for thalidomide families. In the compensation case there were two lists: an X list where it had been proved through medical records that the disabilities were as a result of thalidomide, and a Y list of "maybes." We were on the Y list and had to go to Stirling Hospital to see a thalidomide expert, Dr Spears, so he could assess David.

After examining him, Dr Spears said that the columbine in David's right eye was a trait of Thalidomiders. I was amazed. I said, "Pardon?" He repeated it and I asked him if he was prepared to put that in writing as he was the first doctor who had ever said anything linking his eye to thalidomide. He then said that in his opinion, David was definitely a victim of the drug.

When I heard that, I felt angry that a drug company could produce something that could harm babies, but I felt more angry that our government had let the company carry on marketing the drug after it had already been withdrawn in other countries, and even more angry that the government had never apologised for this to our children and to us.

I never once felt an ounce of guilt. I took something on prescription from a doctor who I thought knew best, for something that was nothing to do with my pregnancy, which happened to harm my baby. No way was it my fault. I have often been asked, if they had had scans then, would I have felt differently about having David but I don't believe I would. I don't believe in abortion for myself, though I don't interfere with anyone else and it is definitely not easy to bring up a disabled child. Your life revolves around them and you can't give your other children the same attention because you have to give it to the disabled baby.

The majority of families were in the same boat as us, without proof that it was thalidomide which caused our children's disabilities, so we had to fight for a slice of the final pot. I flew down to London with two other mothers from Glasgow to see the solicitors who asked us what we were looking for and we said for our children to be provided for during their lifetimes. A few families had already secured a settlement which had been put into trust for them, then the rest of us who numbered around 300, and included David Mason, went en masse to get our claims in.

We had to battle for what we got and that was when the Thalidomide Trust was formed. Eventually, after the campaigns in the press and parliament, we got a decent settlement and the money went into a big pot and was allocated so much per year according to the person's disability. At first we were not very pleased with the arrangement because it felt like having to go cap in hand to ask for the money. People used to have to stipulate what they wanted the money for. In some cases parents spent it on a lavish lifestyle that mostly benefited themselves and it got squandered but we put David's into a property so that we knew he would be secure when we are no longer around.

Now the Thalidomiders get an allocation each year and it's up to them whether they take it all at once or leave it in and take it a bit at a time. The amount of their allocation is decided by the Trust which has a panel of experts who assess the level of disability. Some have very minor problems. Some are deaf with no outer ears, others have short arms, or arms of varying length, some have arms but no legs; not many are partially sighted like David. Many are now beginning to get arthritic pains in their hips – I tease them, saying, "You know what's causing that – old age!" A lot feed themselves with their feet and the wear and tear is beginning to tell on them with aches and pains. David had a hip replacement three years ago.

Some were denied compensation and were left on the Y list but we gradually got them accepted. We still have some Thalidomiders coming forward even now, usually because their parents always denied they were victims of thalidomide but now they have died. They didn't come forward before because they didn't want to upset their parents. I find it very sad that people of nearly 50 have to come along now because their parents were in denial and they have missed out on so much. They have missed joining in with a big, wonderful, inspiring and very special family.

My health visitor recommended I join the Thalidomide Society when David was five because she thought it would be a good idea if I saw how other children like David were coping with their disabilities. I had never seen anyone else like David – all us parents thought we were one-offs – and it came as a bit of a shock to find other children similar. From the start the children connected very closely with each other and it was fascinating to watch them.

My local branch only had half a dozen members but we had an annual Christmas party and summer outing when 30 to 40 Thalidomiders came along with their parents, brothers and sisters so there would be a crowd of a hundred or so. It used to be great fun. Once on our summer outing a man stopped me and said, "I am mesmerized by these children and what they can do. Do you think they will be offended if I bought them icecream?" I said, "Not at all, they would be delighted, go right ahead!"

Other children rarely batted an eyelid when we all showed up. Occasionally at Butlin's you would hear one asking their mum or dad: "Why have those children no arms or legs?" and being told: "Shh, you must not ask questions like that." But we mothers would turn round and tell them it was OK, they could ask whatever they wanted, there was no harm in asking.

These days it is at the Thalidomide Society annual conference that you can see them all behaving as if they belong to the same family. They have all known each other most of their lives and as they arrive the reception rooms echo with endless shouts of greeting and everybody hugs everyone else. They all get cuddles from all the mums too because you feel like you are not just mum to your own but to umpteen others and you are auntie to their kids.

They know each other's disabilities and capabilities and they watch out for each other. You will see them in the bar, one will order drinks but if he or she has no arms to carry them, others will go up and fetch them. They fill in for each other, knowing what each can do but they also have no hesitation about coming to any able-bodied person who happens to be passing for help. I have done all sorts of things for them, including helping people in bathrooms. In some ways, the parents like it because it means they are still needed.

Sometimes I hide away in a corner to watch them all and I feel quite emotional. At night-time the ones who use wheelchairs get on the floor with everyone else to dance. They swing their bodies to the rhythm of the music which pushes their chairs around. When they were teenagers they went through a phase when there was head-banging music – I used to tell them they would suffer later with pains in the neck by shaking their heads around and now some of them are telling me: "You were right!"

When they grew older and had babies of their own, they were so excited to come to the next conference and show them off. I used to watch them change their babies' nappies with their feet and I used to think, if only those doctors who said when you were born that you wouldn't amount to anything could see you now. Some had to go through a lot to have babies, some had IVF, quite a few had caesareans. How the mothers used to manage after having a caesarean section when they couldn't bend over was marvellous to see.

They found ingenious ways round it, just as they have done every problem they have encountered. If there *is* a way round something, they will find it. Many of them put a towel or nappy on the floor, had someone put the baby in the middle, then they collected the four sides of the towel up and lifted the baby with their teeth.

One of the young lads had a fantastic bike with two wheels at the back and one at the front which he lay back on to pedal and steered with his feet but the biggest thing that has amazed me is how many can drive. Many of them drive with their feet, using a steering column on the floor. Others use a steering wheel though that is not so good as it causes a lot of strain round the shoulders.

They started learning to drive when they were 17 or 18 years old and I read an article in the paper about it out to David. It was the only time that he ever mentioned his disability when he said, "I won't ever be able to drive, will I?" I said, "No," and he just said, "Oh well, you will have to keep driving me around then."

My life would have been a much duller existence without my involvement with the Thalidomiders. I would have been one of those housewives quite content to sit back, subservient to the lord and master. But becoming part of the Society spurred me into doing a two-year course at college called Women in Health. It was an assertiveness class on how to bring yourself out and it also included studying influential women from history like Florence Nightingale and the suffragettes. It was fantastic and it gave me the confidence to become chair of the Society.

I have been involved for many years now and whenever I make a speech I always end up by saying to all the Thalidomiders: "You don't know how proud we parents are to have children like you." Every parent is proud of what their children can do but when you have a child with a disability which they have overcome over the years, it makes that pride double.

As well as being chair of the Society, I have been for many years a parent observer on the National Advisory Council for the Thalidomide Trust. I also used to be a volunteer visitor for the Thalidomide Trust, working with beneficiaries who lived at home with elderly parents. I am also involved in a European medical panel concerned with the relicensing of thalidomide mostly to be used to treat multi-myeloma patients.

It is already being used for leprosy which means that in some parts of the world, we are getting new cases of thalidomide babies. For instance, in Brazil it is used without a good safety programme – people are given it appropriately by their doctors but then they share it with other sufferers without realising the dangers.

We are working alongside Pharmion, a pharmaceutical company who want to relicense it. The panel has Thalidomiders from Spain, Sweden and Italy and I am the only non-Thalidomider. We are all trying to work out how a watertight safety procedure can be brought in. I am not against relicensing the drug in principle because for some conditions it is fantastic. For multi-myeloma patients it extends the time and the quality of their lives and who are we to deny patients that? If, out of what people like to call a "tragedy" – though we don't term it as such – could come some good like curing cancer or leprosy, that would be wonderful. I have no objections to it being used for that.

But it has to be dispensed with very stringent controls. It must be properly monitored with a system involving the patient, the doctor and the family. Everything has to be checked, double-checked, triple-checked and signed for. There must be warning signs on the labels, leaflets spelling out why it is not safe for pregnant women. If it is given to a woman of child-bearing age, she should have a pregnancy test every month and use two forms of contraceptive. If a male takes it he should use a condom – no one knows whether it can be passed on through male sperm but we don't want to take any risks.

I think the phenomenon of thalidomide changed pharmaceutical companies for ever. They came up against a force they never reckoned with, the force of thalidomide people who were prepared to do battle with them and make sure they did things differently. If it comes on the market again, we want to guarantee that all the safeguards are in place because we do not want another generation of Thalidomiders.

I have sometimes sat back and thought, what could David have aspired to, if he hadn't been disabled? (I never say, even to myself, "not normal" because he is normal.) What could he have achieved? Then I think it's daft looking at it that way. Instead I should look at what he *has* achieved which is a full and happy life. He has two nieces and five nephews who think the world of him. They all used to do things to help Uncle David, whether he wanted to be helped or not. None of them were ever rude or nasty to him.

Everybody round here knows David who is the only Thalidomider in Barnsley, so far as we know. I don't know half the neighbours, but they all know him and know me just as David's mum. He's got so many people looking out for him that if he was in town and there was any trouble going on, people would surround him and protect him.

Through my connection with Thalidomiders, I have grown a lot as a person; it has really enriched my life. After the Women in Health course, I was able to do public speaking – before that I would never have stood up. I became acting chair of the Thalidomide Society in November, 2002, and chair in March, 2003. At the conference that year, I was shaking like a leaf before I started speaking but when I'd finished someone proposed a vote of thanks to me and they all applauded. I felt wonderful.

I have met hundreds of people over the years, Thalidomiders and their families. My eldest grand-daughter still goes to the conferences because she has made friends with many of the Thalidomiders' children, so the special family has over the years grown into a huge extended one.

Hopefully there will never be another family like it even

though it has been a hugely enriching experience to be part of it. People ask me why I am still involved at over 65; it's because I love doing it. I just love being involved with them all. I have never ever seen another group of people interacting together as closely as they do.

One characteristic that unites them is determination. Every one of them is determined – whatever they set out to do, they are determined to succeed. Another way of putting that is to say they are extremely stubborn; and I have always said they have needed to be in order to get through life the way they are. I admire them all; they are the gutsiest lot of people going.

Chapter Thirteen
Darren And Me

WHEN I LEFT CHAILEY in 1979 I went to spend the first two weeks of the summer holidays in a hotel in Jersey which was owned by the Thalidomide Trust and where we all used to get together to let our hair down on what was known as "mad fortnight" when it was a case of "anything goes". It was very nice to have this facility where we were all in the same boat and we could go to the beach without feeling self-conscious, particularly when we were teenagers.

One of the high spots of a trip to Jersey in those years was our nights out to Caesar's Palace nightclub and cabaret and I'd been there three or four days when one of these was scheduled. Around 18 of us were going with our carers and we had a mini-bus but it would only fit three wheelchairs and we had four.

The lightest and most able were asked to get out of their wheelchairs and as I was pretty agile, I got out of mine and found a seat at the side of the bus next to a good looking 18-year-old called Darren Mansell. He had these really sapphire-blue eyes and when they looked into mine, they were just gorgeous and I got butterflies in my tummy. He also had the most fabulous bum in the world and footballers' muscular legs. He had a gorgeous smile as well and the fact that he looked at me without seeing my body, that he looked at the person within, made it extra special.

We had a great night at Caesar's though I have to confess I drank a little bit too much of a lurid-coloured cocktail called a

Blue Lagoon, made of Cointreau, lemonade and lime. But we were chatting away and getting on very well. On the way back the mini-bus driver told Darren to keep hold of me so I wouldn't topple over but actually I was propping him up as there was no way he could hold on to me because he was more drunk than I was and had no idea what he was doing.

When we got back to the hotel he gave me a peck on the cheek to say goodnight. I knew there had been a real chemical reaction between us so the next morning the first thing I did was knock on his door to tell him to come for breakfast with me. Luckily, I didn't suffer from shyness when it came to getting on with boys!

Over the next couple of days we spent most of our time together and, as we got to know each other, we found we never stopped chatting about every subject under the sun. There was definitely love there from the beginning, we really gelled. I went to his room for a kiss and a cuddle, as you do, and by the time he went home we had made plans to see each other as often as we could.

Darren was born on April 9, 1961 at Hallam Hospital in West Bromwich, West Midlands, the son of Stan and June Mansell, who had taken Distaval during her pregnancy for morning sickness. Just like my mum, his mother was prevented from seeing him for the first four days of his life but when she lost her temper and demanded they bring her baby to her, the nurses relented.

Though Darren was born with no arms, it never occurred to the Mansells not to take him home to the house they shared with his mum's parents whom he called Nanny Allen and Grandad George.

Darren

My dad had two brothers and a sister and my mum was the youngest of ten children, so I had lots of aunts and uncles. Unfortunately, my parents never had any more children so I was an only child but I had loads of cousins living in the area who were just the same as brothers and sisters.

I had Black Country grandparents who were totally

supportive from day one. I had a special relationship with my mum's mother, Nanny Allen, who was a larger than life woman, having had ten children, and could take anything in her stride. I remember her rubbing my short arms and advising me: "Make the most of what you've got." She used to make traditional bread pudding and I was a devil sticking my thumb into the butter.

Their house was next to the Baker family who had a girl of my age called Angela and we played together in the back yard. As I learnt to walk, my nose took a battering and I am told it broke about 20 times but she, like my cousins, treated me no differently to any other kid, playing rough and tumble, football and everything that children did.

My other nan was Nan Mansell who lived in Dudley where my Dad came from and she was a very petite lady. My granddad was called Grandee who was a baker and made pikelets and cakes.

I learned to feed and dress myself through getting aids and instruction at Queen Mary's Hospital at Roehampton and watching how other children managed. My family gave me a lot of encouragement by telling me that I had to find a way to do things as they were not always going to be there to do them for me.

I had a little ring in my trouser zip which I pulled up with a dressing stick and my clothes had a lot of Velcro. I have got quite good dexterity with my arms and I learned to eat with a fork and a long-handled spoon. I had to sit down with the family at mealtimes and get on with it. Nowadays I don't feel the need to prove myself to be completely independent. If I'm in a restaurant and order a steak, I ask the chef to cut it up rather than spend ten minutes wrestling with it myself.

My dad became the Midlands chairman of the Thalidomide Society which helped the victims of thalidomide before we got the compensation. From the beginning he campaigned hard for proper compensation along with Sylvia and Len Williams who had thalidomide twins, Peter and Andrew. We went on quite a lot of trips where we met other Thalidomiders and their parents, for instance to the pantomime where we met the stars after the performance. From those early days I felt part of the thalidomide "family" which exists to this day.

When I was five years old we moved to our own ground-floor maisonette. My parents worked in the daytime so I was left in the morning at Nanny Allen's from where I was picked up for school. This is where my liking for chocolate came from as my grandmother always got me either a Turkish Delight or a Bar Six to take to school.

It was decided that I would go to the Wilson Stuart School which was on a three-part campus consisting of a physically handicapped, a blind and a deaf school. I remember it being very much a disabled environment. The Williams twins went there together with Melvyn, another thalidomide lad from West Bromwich. We used to play football outside with our sticks, crutches and legs all going everywhere in our enthusiasm for the game.

One of the most boring aspects of those days was having to spend hours in front of ultra-violet lamps because I had some health problems which the doctor said was caused by my not getting enough sun. I also hated wearing my artificial arms which I was forced to do all the time I was at school. I used to "gas" people with the powered arms if they annoyed me.

As I was coming up to eleven my parents wanted me to go to mainstream school. I passed the 11 Plus examination and went for a meeting at Menzies High School in West Bromwich which several of my cousins already attended. The head teacher was against me going but we had the wholehearted backing of his deputy and I got in mainly because my cousins were there. I was probably one of the pioneers of disabled children going to "normal" school. Thankfully, they allowed me to give up my artificial arms.

I now have a good job as a Finance Officer with the West Midlands Police. The people I work with are brilliant. They treat me as an equal and we bounce off each other. I crack all the politically incorrect disabled jokes and they say, "Only you could get away with saying that!" We push the boundaries sometimes but we are a happy bunch.

I love football and have spent a lot of my leisure time as a referee, working my way up to becoming semi-professional in the Midlands Football Combination.

Socially, I was quite shy as a teenager until I was 17 and got some money from the Thalidomide Trust. I didn't have a real girlfriend until I met Louise. She was my first proper girlfriend.

Louise

After Darren and I said goodbye to each other at the end of our holiday in Jersey I didn't see him for three or four weeks but soon after I started at the Star Centre in Cheltenham he began driving down to visit me after football matches every other Saturday.

I would start tarting myself up at about 4 p.m. though he wasn't due to arrive until 8 p.m. I would have a shower and try to eat something though I usually couldn't manage it as my stomach was in knots. I used to count the minutes while telling myself he was bound to be late because he was always late. By 7.30 p.m. I'd be sitting eagerly waiting for him and when he arrived it was like all the butterflies in the whole world were fluttering about in my stomach.

It was a really lovely feeling to see him walking towards me. All I wanted to do was to run, well, wheel, and give him a hug but obviously if I zoomed up to him in my chair I would probably have run him over so I had to restrain myself.

There was usually a disco on which I had organised as vice-president of the students' union so we would go to that, have a drink and a dance and go back to my room. We weren't supposed to have guests in the rooms so we would have to sneak in to make sure none of the care staff spotted us. The next day he would be up and gone by 7 a.m. to get to his Sunday football match.

The weekends he didn't come down, I went up to his house, skipping the last lecture to get the train on the Friday afternoon. In those days trains didn't have disabled access and you had to sit in the guard's van. I travelled with bags of post, bicycles, dogs, snakes in baskets, shut in a kind of wire cage. It was very cold but ridiculously cheap as I was classed as cargo.

At the station Darren would be waiting for me with his dad who put my wheelchair in the car and took me to his house. Darren always went to his parents' for meals which I found strange because he had his own beautiful house. Though it was just a house, not a home. There was nothing personal in it. He even had plastic on the floor to protect the carpet and he ordered me to keep to it in my wheelchair. When he wasn't looking I used to sneak my wheels off the plastic, just because he told me not to.

Because I only saw Darren for short periods I occasionally had other boyfriends. One was a police trainee who came to the Star Centre to do his community service. I think I was attracted to him because of his uniform. I love uniforms. Anyway, we hit it off and went out for about two weeks.

Then there was Andrew Hitchman, a fellow student who was in the later stages of muscular dystrophy. He had nice eyes, like Darren. At Christmas in my first year he invited me to go to his home in Wales but I turned him down as I had already arranged to go to Walsingham.

The muscles were deteriorating in his chest and he had a continuous cough. The doctor said there was nothing he could do except to eat Polo mints to freshen his breath. I phoned every other day to see how he was and the day after New Year's Day they told me he had died in his sleep.

Because of his lungs, he couldn't lie down but slept sitting up supported by pillows. That night before going to bed he had said goodbye to everyone as if he knew he was dying. They looked in on him at about 1 a.m. and saw him sitting up but when they went to wake him at 8 a.m., he was cold. The postmortem showed he had died at about 1 a.m. so when they had looked in on him, he had probably already gone.

I also went out for about three weeks with Steve Thomas who had spina bifida. He was built like a rugby player and would have been about 6ft tall if he had stood up. One day he went all romantic and wanted to have sex with me. I said no, whereupon he threw me off the bed. Literally, just pushed me off. So that finished abruptly.

I left the Star Centre in July, 1981 by which time I had bought my house and Darren came to stay most Saturday nights. That Christmas I still could not go to my own family so Darren invited me to his. I had only just passed my driving test and had my Mini Clubman which slewed around all over the place when it hit even a tiny bit of ice and the day I was to drive to his there was a big snowfall.

On the way to Darren's I called in on a college friend who lived up a hill in Handsworth and when I left his place my car slid sideways, all the way down the slope with me panicking behind the wheel not knowing what to do. Luckily I didn't hit any other cars but by the time I got to Darren's I was a nervous wreck and badly in need of the cup of tea his mum offered me.

His dad very kindly always checked my tyres, water and oil and, if the car was particularly dirty, he would wash it. They gave me Darren's bed while he slept on the settee. His dad used to carry me upstairs and he put a chair in front of the toilet so I could get on and off by myself. Then I would bump downstairs on my front.

On Christmas Eve we all went to the pub where the men went up to the bar while the women were left sitting round the table, which I found really strange. I hardly knew any of the women and I thought, I didn't come to the pub to be with them, I came to be with Darren, so I didn't like that very much.

The next day we ate Christmas dinner, then it was back to the pub. I was used to a more formal Christmas at my parents', opening presents together in the morning, the dinner with all the trimmings, then listening to the Queen's speech. It was good to see how others celebrated Christmas and they were both nice in their different ways.

Seeing Darren for more than just a few hours for once meant we bonded much more strongly and when I left, it was a real wrench. He asked me if I would consider moving to Birmingham and I said, no, would he move to Cheltenham? That wasn't on either because he said his life was up there.

The following May we were in bed one morning at my

house when I noticed him looking happy yet anxious. I thought it was something to do with football until he said what was on his mind. "Would you marry me?" he asked, casually, in the same tone as he might have said, "Would you like a piece of chocolate?" There were no romantic preliminaries or going down on one knee.

So I took it pretty casually too and said no, I was too young – I was still only 19 – and was just settling in to my own house. He wanted me to move in with him in Birmingham but I had only just left institutional life and discovered personal space and freedom for the first time and I just wasn't ready to give it up. I expected him to wait a while and ask me again when I was ready and for a time we carried on the same. I went to training college in Leatherhead, Surrey, but still saw him at weekends and rang him every other day in the week.

Not long afterwards he missed a couple of weekends because of football so the next time he was coming I got really excited. He had been going on a lot about seeing what I looked like on my artificial legs. I hadn't worn them for ages but to please him I got them down from the loft and strapped them on in the afternoon so I could walk around for a couple of hours to get accustomed to them again.

I was watching out for him coming down the drive because I wanted to see the expression on his face when he first saw me on the legs. The time came for him to arrive and he didn't turn up, which was a huge disappointment. I rang his home and he said he couldn't come because his aunt had died so I phoned his mum and dad to pass on my condolences and his dad said, "What aunt? She's still alive."

I was extremely upset that he had lied to me, especially as I had made a really big effort, put my hated legs on and cooked his favourite meal. I threw off the legs, went out to the pub and got drunk. On the Monday I rang him as usual and his mum told me he was not there. On Wednesday it was the same story by which time I was beginning to smell a rat. But I trusted him completely and it never occurred to me that he might cheat on me, fool that I was, especially as he had only recently asked me to marry him. I didn't think he was the type.

The following weekend I had invited John home from college, just as a friend, and had told him Darren would be there. When I phoned Darren on the Friday at his mum's where he spent most of his time and he wasn't there again, she suggested I try his own house. So I did and a woman answered.

She said, "Who should I say it is?" and I replied, "It's his girlfriend." She retorted, "Oh no, you can't be his girlfriend. I've been his girlfriend for a month." I said, "Well, I've been his girlfriend for two and a half years and a month ago he asked me to marry him." She said, "Hang on," and yelled, "Darren!"

When he picked up the phone I asked, "Who's that?" "Oh, a friend," he said, at which point I heard the other phone being slammed down. I said, "If you are downstairs, she must be upstairs. In your bedroom. She says she's been your girlfriend for a month, is that right?" He said, "Sort of."

I decided to put a stop to this so I said, "It's finished for us, then?" He said, "No," but I replied, "Oh, yes it is, because I am dumping you and, anyway I have got another man here." That got him riled up and he said he was going to come down and "smash his head open with a milk bottle". I said, "I wouldn't bother, Darren. He's got two arms and two legs and he will beat you up."

I felt totally gutted and really angry. That was the end as far as I was concerned. I never expected to hear from Darren again.

Darren

I've loved Louise since we first met in Jersey. In hindsight, it was sensible for her to turn down my marriage proposal as we were both very young, but maybe I should then have stuck with it a bit more. Instead, I gave up on her and I married Gill on July 14, 1984. Our daughter Stacey arrived the following July and Natalie was born in July, 1989. Despite our marital difficulties, the girls have both grown up to be great kids. They were fiercely defensive of me when we went out as a family, particularly Natalie. If another kid said, "He's got no arms," she would go straight over and say, "It's not his fault," and explain about thalidomide.

Around the time my first marriage broke up I became curious about what had happened to Lou and decided to send a Christmas card to her via the Thalidomide Trust. She got in touch with me and we spoke two or three times on the phone, then met up and it was just like before. We hit it off straight away. We had the same connection we always had.

Louise

It was Christmas, 2000, when Darren's card arrived saying that as we Thalidomiders get older, we should keep in touch. As soon as I saw his name my heart started thumping in that old familiar way. I plucked up the courage to ring him, Gill answered and I gave my married name and I don't think she made the connection. I thought it would be a five-minute call to catch up but we were on the phone for an hour and a half, chatting away about our lives with the same ease as before.

A couple of days later we talked again and he asked if he could come to meet me on the Saturday. As soon as he got out of the car, I was struck once more by those gorgeous sapphire-blue eyes. But I was still angry about what he had done to me and I thought, right, I'm going to get him back for that.

He stayed for three or four hours and the whole time I was really hard on him. I was quite nasty to him, very catty. I put him through the mill so much I thought it would be the last I saw of him. When it was time to say goodbye he leaned over and gave me the most wonderful kiss I had had in a long, long time and my heart started to go boom-a-boom. Then he just looked at me and said, "I love you." That was it. I was hooked.

The next day he rang in the afternoon and again in the evening, and the next day and the next and the next and at the weekend he came down on the Sunday. It was strange because we just picked up exactly where we had left off. It was as if we hadn't been apart from each other all those years.

He didn't talk about problems in his marriage, except to say that he and Gill were not getting on, but it was somehow understood that we would keep our relationship secret. I hated it being secret: I wanted to shout it out to the world. I also felt very bad about going out with Darren when he was still married as it was exactly what John had done to me. He told me he wanted to move in with me which I wasn't comfortable with as it made me feel like a mistress even though Thalidomider friends told me that he and his wife had not been happy together for about nine years.

After three or four months we had got so close we were talking to each other two or three times a day and seeing each other every week and it was heart-wrenching every time he went home and really joyful every time he came. Then one day he suddenly went very cold. I asked him what was wrong but he wouldn't tell me.

The next day he phoned and said he had been thinking about where our relationship was going and had decided to give his marriage another chance. Unknown to him, I was feeling extremely low that day because I was ill with my kidney problem and I had just heard that John's mum had died. Even though she didn't like me at first, I had grown fond of her and John was absolutely devastated. The children loved their nan very much, she reminded me of the way my nan was to me. She used to come once a month to look after them so I was trying to console them all while feeling dreadful myself.

Listening to Darren, I felt my heart breaking. Just as I thought my life had picked up, that someone loved me again for who I was, after John had shoved me down to the ground and stamped on me, my world was falling apart. It almost pushed me over the edge.

I thought, the only way I can cope with this is to leave the kids and go off on my own for a drive. So I got in the car and drove up the hill to a place called Fox Cote where there is a sheer drop down a cliff face. I felt so miserable I thought, I'm going to throw myself off this cliff.

As I was sitting there, staring gloomily out over the drop, Darren phoned and I told him what I was thinking. He kept on talking to me, saying over and over, "You don't want to do that." As soon as he put the phone down, the kids rang and said, "When are you coming home to make our tea?" So, obviously, I would have to leave jumping off the cliff to another day. I went home for tea instead and that little cupboard inside of me opened just enough for me to stuff the hurt feeling in so I could cope.

I moped for a long while, wishing the phone to ring. The kids were very supportive, as was John who cursed Darren up and down for treating me badly. Then my transplant came up and when I recovered I had a lot going on with the Woodcraft Folk so I kept busy. I respected and accepted Darren's decision as well and thought that he and I were just not meant to be. Three years went by without any contact, then in March, 2005, I decided to go with Jack to the Thalidomide Society's 40th anniversary celebration in Bromborough, near Birkenhead.

Darren was there; I saw him walk past before he saw me and my heart started that old familiar thumping. He spotted me and invited me to look at a DVD the Society had made giving advice to families in Brazil, where thalidomide victims are still being born, about washing and dressing and so on. I went with him and he kissed me. We spent the rest of the weekend together and it all started up again between us.

Jack remembered how hurt I'd been so he didn't like Darren one bit. As we were leaving, Jack said, "You've got to keep away from that man, he'll hurt you again," and whenever Darren rang, Jack would shout, "Tell him to stay with his wife." It took quite some time before he forgave him.

I insisted to Darren that this time our relationship could not be a secret. He had to make his mind up who he wanted, me or Gill; he couldn't have both. And I told him he would have to prove his commitment to me before I could trust him again. He promised faithfully he would tell Gill about us but he still dithered until she found out anyway when she caught him chatting with me on the internet.

I invited him to move in with me but he still wouldn't make up his mind, telling me he needed a couple of weeks to think about it. In the meantime, I had got to know another Thalidomider called Steve, from Scotland, and had formed a jokey relationship with him over the internet. I must admit, I am a flirt, so I was flirting madly with him online and I also arranged to meet him in Edinburgh when I was there delivering a lecture.

Darren was getting more and more jealous and suspicious. He felt threatened and afraid that he might lose me again. Steve decided to exploit this so he would ring me at 11 p.m. and not put the phone down until 1 a.m. so that Darren could never get through. He got to the stage of asking me, if I wasn't with Darren, would I move up to Scotland? I said, if I wasn't with Darren, would he move down to Cheltenham? Neither of us was prepared to move, so that was it, but we kept on chatting.

One weekend there was a big international Woodcraft camp in Sherwood Forest and Darren decided to come along. I'll never forget seeing him marching in with his eyes wide open, his head up and his chest puffed out. You know how a man pumps himself up if he wants to be serious, like a knight in shining armour? If he had had arms, his muscles would have been bulging and flexing.

He stalked into my tent and demanded, "Tell me, are you serious about Steve or is it me you want? I have to know." I said, "Well, I want you, but what do you want? Because every time I say come and live with me you find some excuse."

So finally he made up his mind to move in with me and he arrived on August 13, 2005. It was absolute chaos at first and quite a hard adjustment to make, especially for the children. The day before he was coming, I thought, oh my God, have I made the right decision? I had been on my own for 12 years, done what I wanted, when I wanted and I didn't have to be answerable to anyone.

Sharing the house with two carers was already sometimes a bit of a strain and to have another person there might make it worse. He's very neat and particular about everything while I'm a mischievous person and a practical joker. On April Fool's Day, I'm the type who will put cling film over the toilets and string cotton thread across doorways. One first of April I added food dye to the shower gel which Darren puts on a brush to wash himself. When he looked down at his feet, they had turned blue.

He absolutely hates frogs and once the kids found out, they knew how to torture him. Jack got hold of the big leafy bit of a tomato plant, hid it in his hand and shook it in Darren's face, yelling gleefully, "Look at this frog!" You have never seen anyone jump on the settee so quickly! I was killing myself laughing while Darren was going totally loopy. Another time, I got a plastic frog, put it in an envelope and sent it to him at work. His friend opened it and this frog jumped out. She had a phobia about them too and she nearly had a heart attack.

One Valentine's Day, I sent him a single rose at work with a card sprayed with perfume. When it was delivered the reception announced, "Would Mr Mansell please come and collect his rose." He was so embarrassed he got really angry so the next year I sent him some balloons. Last year for April Fool I put a stitch in his work trousers so he couldn't get his foot in and inserted a whistle up his car exhaust. I am always playing jokes and messing around like this. He calls me a big kid at times.

His little routines still annoy me. For instance, his socks have the names of the days of the week stitched into them and have to be stacked in a certain order in the drawer. That drove me so mad one day that I got them all out and matched a Thursday with a Tuesday, a Monday with a Wednesday. He had to sort them all back in the right pairs and days. He said, "I really hate that," and I said, "You shouldn't be so finicky."

I was fearful at first that he might try to control me, as John did. Anyway, I took a gamble but, determined to start as I meant to go on, I made it clear that, no matter how hard he pushed, I would not be controlled. We would have to resolve any conflicts by negotiation. The fear lasted for the first nine months and he did once try to tell me how to treat the carers. I think I am a fair employer but it's really difficult when you have got people living in your house and working for you, they can't become your friends. So when I ask for something to be done that is part of their job and they give me a mouthful, I come down on them hard.

Darren didn't like it and told me I should not treat people like that, so we negotiated that, as far as the carers are concerned, they are mine. I am their employer and I will tell them what needs to be done, where, when and how, and he should stay out of it.

We argue a lot but we also get on really well and have a lot of fun so when Darren's divorce was going ahead, we started talking about marriage. I spotted a ring in a shop which I really loved so we bought it but I said I wouldn't wear it until he actually got down on his knees and proposed properly. It stayed in the safe while we continued to discuss whether we needed and wanted to get married.

I felt sure he was going to ask me before we went on holiday to Tenerife at Christmas, 2007 with Emma and Jack and my two carers. But he didn't so I stopped thinking about it. I took some tinsel with me to make our hotel rooms look Christmassy and I borrowed one of the little plastic conifer trees they were using as table decorations in the restaurant for us to put our presents round. It was too small for the presents to fit under so we stuck it on a beer can and covered the can in tinsel.

After breakfast on Christmas morning we all opened our presents until we got down to the last one, an oblong package with tinsel wrapped round it which my carer, Maria, said was for me. I knew it was from Darren so I opened it and found a box saying sun-tan lotion. I had already got at least three bottles of varying degrees of protection so I thought, why would I want more sun-tan lotion? But I politely said, "Oh, that's nice. Thank you very much."

Then he told me to open the box, so I did and found it packed with toilet paper which I pulled out bit by bit, finding nothing until I got right to the bottom where there was a small parcel wrapped up in more toilet paper. I unwrapped that and saw it was a ring box but before I could open it, Darren took it off me, went down on his knees, showed me the lovely ring and said, "Louise, will you marry me?" It turned out that he had got the ring out of the safe without me knowing and brought it to Tenerife hidden in Maria's suitcase so he could surprise me.

We had talked over various scenarios for the proposal and, to my mind, this was the perfect one: on a special day and in front of the kids so that they could see that Darren really wanted me. It took me a long time – at least five seconds – to say "Yes!!" Then for the rest of the day I went round announcing the news to everyone I saw, the staff in reception, guests in the hotel, anyone who passed by: "Look, I got engaged today!" and flashing my ring. The kids were happy too because they knew now that Darren wasn't going to be here today, gone tomorrow. This was permanent.

I know that, having been brought up in Chailey without a parent's love and cuddles, there are some things I do which are single-minded and institutionalised still and I'm sure Darren would agree. But three years after we started living together, he and I are very, very happy. I love him to bits.

Darren

Now Lou and I go everywhere together – to formal dinners, up to London to the shops and restaurants, off on holiday. We still sometimes battle with accessibility but we just get on with it. On holiday the kids go swimming or water skiing and we just walk around together and we love it.

Lou is very stubborn and headstrong, very much a leader, which suits me. I like someone who is decisive. But she likes spontaneity whereas I prefer structure. I like to be told on Monday what we are doing on Friday and to have it down on a calendar. We do bicker about not putting things on the calendar. So there are days when we are happy families and others when we are at war with each other. Some days are tough, others brilliant, just like in any family.

I think Lou is remarkable for what she does. I say to her that I will probably pop my clogs before her as I don't exercise a lot since I gave up refereeing. But we face each day as it comes. That's what it's all about: going through the good times and the bad times, together.

Chapter Fourteen
Wedding Bells

I WAS BLISSFULLY HAPPY that Darren and I had now committed ourselves to getting married and being together for the rest of our lives. I felt settled, secure, and very much in love. My parents were really happy at the news, in fact I later found out that Darren had asked their permission to marry me on a visit down for Sunday dinner. But though everything seemed sunny, unbeknown to me a little cloud was gathering on the horizon. It was soon to turn into a full-scale thunderstorm and burst with spectacular force over my head.

Through my various activities, particularly the Woodcraft Folk and my campaigns for access to public buildings for disabled people, I am quite well known in Cheltenham and over the years have been treated as a bit of a celebrity by the local paper, the *Gloucestershire Echo*. So when I got back from holiday and started telling everyone I knew about our engagement, the paper soon got wind of it and asked if they could do a happy story on us.

I could not see why not, especially as the paper had backed my access campaigns in the past. I didn't expect the rest of my family to see the story as it was only going to be printed locally and, anyway, it could not do anyone any harm.

So they did a short interview and printed a joyful, laughing picture of the two of us on the front page and another picture on page three with about 20 paragraphs saying "Cheltenham couple Darren Mansell and Louise Medus have overcome the odds to find true love." It went on to say: "They were reunited four years ago after more than two decades apart and Louise says she could not be happier. Darren is marrying the love of his life, Louise, 27 years after he first popped the big question."

I thought it was lovely but my ex-husband, John, took it upon himself to cut it out and send it to my parents accompanied by a letter expressing his "unhappiness and concern regarding Louise's obvious obsession with publicity and the damage this is having on our children".

He said that, since December, 2007, I had appeared in the *Gloucestershire Echo* at least three times "winging (sic – he meant whingeing) about various things", accused me of "constant attention seeking" and said it was "unhealthy for Jack".

At the time I was merrily discussing with Darren how many people we were going to invite to our wedding, looking for venues for the ceremony and dreaming up ideas for my perfect dress and I knew nothing of John's action until I got an extremely upsetting letter from my dad two weeks later, enclosing a copy of John's letter to him and saying that he agreed "with every point that he makes".

I could barely believe what I was reading as the letter went on to say that he had "read with dismay the disgraceful article" in the *Echo* which he had found to be "obscene, untruthful and … a disgrace." He said the article was "trashy and self-congratulatory," accused me of having an "obvious obsession with publicity" and said "you should be ashamed of yourself".

He also complained that the article implied that I had been "dumped in an institution" and that this was not true. But it is a fact. I was not abandoned by my family, but I was dumped. Not only that, but I had recently received my records from Chailey Heritage and I was cut to the quick when I read a report saying that, after my birth, my parents had sent a letter requesting that I come two weeks earlier than the date they had been given to take me there, so that they could go on holiday.

My aunt had always told me that my parents didn't want me to go to a home, but they could see no alternative. So I was shocked and upset to learn that in fact they had asked Chailey to take me two weeks early.

About the wedding, my father wrote that it was usual with

a second marriage for there to be a registry office ceremony followed by a family lunch, "but I now realise that you are planning a full-blown jamboree with all and sundry and quite obviously the participation of the press and I want you to know that your mother and I will therefore not be attending". He would only come, he said, if Darren and I decided to have a registry office wedding "with a <u>private</u> family lunch" afterwards.

I felt completely gutted because I knew that when he said he wasn't going to come, he would not come. Years previously we had fallen out just before Jack's christening, again over me appearing in the press. I had been complaining about accessibility and my dad had gone loopy about it and told me he would not attend the christening. I kept thinking, he doesn't really mean it. He wouldn't miss his own grandson's christening, but, sure enough, he didn't come.

I sat there with the letter in my hand and cried. It broke my heart. I have always felt intimidated by my father and he rules the rest of the family too. What he says goes and if you go against it, God help you. And when Dad sends you to Coventry, he sends you to Coventry in Australia. You are way, way out; he doesn't talk about you or ask anyone how you are, your name is unmentionable.

I was unbelievably upset. I started saying I wouldn't get married at all if I couldn't have his blessing on my happiness. I couldn't believe that he could be so cruel, especially in the light of him saying that, if I would only organise the kind of occasion he thought I should have, then he would come.

I know he doesn't like publicity, except when it suits him – a year previously he had been running a campaign to improve the kidney transplant service in Oxford and I found myself talked about in *The Sunday Times* without anyone asking my permission. And it is true, as he said in the letter, that I had once promised him not to go in the press any more.

But I am 46 years old, a middle-aged woman with my own independent life. I didn't see why I should have to ask permission from my father to appear in a newspaper talking about my life, though in actual fact I never had any intention to invite the press to my wedding. I am a disability rights campaigner and as such am a public figure in a minor way and my main weapon is publicity. For instance, I am involved in a campaign to get compensation for thalidomide victims in countries where it has never even been acknowledged that the drug was used, like Italy and Spain or where the amount awarded was very low, like Germany, and the main tactic is to hold demonstrations to attract publicity. Also, I knew I was writing this book so if I'd promised not to go in the papers again; I would have been an appalling hypocrite.

It is also true that Jack doesn't like it when my being in the paper makes people talk about me at school. He is a teenage boy, easily embarrassed, and it is understandable. On the other hand Emma is very supportive. But I have sat down with him and explained how I need publicity for my campaigns, and he is all right with it.

I was in a dreadful quandary because I really wanted my dad to be at the wedding. Darren and I wanted the day to be fun and relaxed after a formal start. We had planned that my father should give me away, my brother, David, should be an usher with Jack, my sister Lindsey was to do one of the readings at the ceremony, and a cousin the other, and my niece should join Emma and Darren's daughters as bridesmaids. After the ceremony we planned to have a buffet meal for 100 family and friends, followed by dancing to a band and a disco.

Now we were faced with the dilemma that, however much I wanted my father there, the price we had to pay was that we couldn't have the kind of wedding we wanted. We decided that price was too high. One by one the rest of the family rang me up to say they had heard I'd fallen out with Dad who wasn't coming to the wedding unless I apologised and stopped going in the press, and they weren't coming either because I had offended my father.

I couldn't see what I had to apologise for but I still hoped to find a way out of this situation. My brother and my aunts agreed that I had the right to do what I wanted but they warned me that the consequences would be high. One cousin said if I didn't do what my father wanted I would regret it, another said he could see both sides but as his parents were not coming, he could not come.

We still sent invitations to all of them and I pleaded with my dad on the phone, saying "Please, please, please come. It won't be the same without you." Every time I spoke to them it really did cut me up, it was excruciating. My kids couldn't understand why they were not coming. Emma said, should she have a word with Granddad? I said no, because he would probably disown her too.

After a lot of pleading my brother and sister, Claire, agreed to put pressure on my parents and my aunts said they wanted to attend if they could, so at last I felt people were rallying round when another bombshell broke. Back in January the *Daily Mail* had picked up the *Gloucestershire Echo* story and did a short interview with us which I agreed to so long as they did not ask me about my family.

It had not been printed and I forgot about it. Then on April 23rd Darren and I were on a train going to London to meet a potential fundraiser for an event we are planning in 2012 to commemorate the 50th anniversary of the date when the government ordered all old stocks of thalidomide to be destroyed, meaning that no more British thalidomide babies would be born, when we got a phone call from a friend saying I was in the *Daily Mail*.

Darren jumped off the train at Swindon to grab a paper, and there we were on a double-page spread. It was quite frightening. Then the "This Morning" programme rang inviting us to go on to talk about the Thalidomiders round the world who hadn't got compensation and our plans for demonstrations outside the German embassy to pressurise their government to act.

There was nothing negative in either the article or the TV interview, I didn't talk about my childhood but about what is happening now. Yet John wrote again to my dad saying I was upsetting Jack and my dad hit the roof.

He shouted down the phone at me about how dare I go in the press to talk about thalidomide? I said, "Dad, that is exactly what you did!" He ranted on that he had had enough, he wanted no more to do with thalidomide, ever. This was the final insult and he definitely would not come to the wedding.

All my relatives then rang me up again saying they would not come to the wedding either because I had offended my parents or because they didn't want to fall out with my dad. So I wrote a letter to my father explaining why I did what I did and sent a copy of it to everyone else in the family. That may have been wrong; I should probably have kept it between us, but he had dragged everyone into it and I felt I needed to have my say.

I apologised for the hurt I caused by, in his view, implying that I had been dumped, but pointed out that in his own book he had related how I had been sent to a residential school and hospital for disabled children and spent little time at home. I explained the article was done to commemorate the 50th anniversary of thalidomide going on sale in the UK. I told him I was "shocked and hurt" that he paid attention to what John wrote as he had "mentally abused me and committed adultery (with my own care workers) to such an extent that I felt my life was not worth living. He continually sponged off my money (and yours)."

I went on, "I know my publicity and my media exposure upsets you, but it is about me, not you. The letter you sent me is not how a letter from a father should be. Your anger comes through too strongly for that. I felt really hurt that you could have written such a letter. As you say, I am coming into my middle-age. I expect to run my own life. It is time that you start to treat me as an adult, and not as a child. Had I not been affected by thalidomide, I know that I would have succeeded in business, and been even more financially independent than I am now.

"Both Darren and I would love you both to come to the wedding. If you choose not to attend, that is your decision, but both Emma and Jack will be very hurt. I am astonished to learn that you appear to have put pressure on the rest of the family to the extent that they are thinking of not coming to this family occasion.

"Saying that I am not taking proper care of my children

and their interests is total rubbish. I love my children more than anything and I won't let them be hurt or treated badly in any way. I will not put them through what I went through: one minute being treated as part of the family and then dropped the next."

While all this was going on, our plans were progressing for the wedding. As soon as we got engaged we went round looking at venues and going to wedding fairs. We had decided not to get married in Cheltenham because of John writing that letter – we had told him he was not welcome at the wedding but were afraid he might still turn up and cause a scene.

The only Saturday we could do it was August 30th because Emma was working in an American children's camp, called Tripp Lake Camp, the whole summer and the first place we liked didn't have that date free. At our third or fourth wedding fair, when we were beginning to get a bit despondent about finding the right venue, we started chatting to a toastmaster and asked him if he knew of anywhere which would fit our requirements: somewhere with a wedding licence which was simple but classier than a village hall and yet not a hotel.

He told us of a 300-year-old barn near Newent, Gloucestershire, called The Dark Barn. It was not far so we went to look and, even though it was closed, we fell in love with it straight away. It was in the middle of nowhere, as classy as a church, with a beautiful lake outside with a bridge going over it which was perfect for photographs.

We arranged to visit the next day and were shown the bedrooms which had been converted from stables. They had two disabled room but the other rooms were also accessible and the bridal suite had a four-poster bed but no top. Right next to it was a huge white marquee where we could have the reception.

The people were lovely and they served Darren's favourite cider, so he was happy. We decided on a buffet with those in wheelchairs being served by the staff so they didn't have to struggle, and we booked it there and then for 100 people.

Next I had to find the perfect dress. I went to wedding shops initially looking for a head dress. I didn't want a veil as I didn't think it appropriate for a second marriage and Darren would not have been able to lift it up – we had to be practical as well as romantic – but I wanted something nice in my hair. In the end my Auntie Hilary made me two tiaras and two hair combs to go in my hair but at one wedding fair I asked various people if they knew of a good wedding-dress maker.

I knew I wanted a long dress which was suitable for wearing in a wheelchair and I didn't want to buy a dress and have it adapted, because I had my own ideas. Somebody told me of a lady called Nina who had a shop near me so I went to see her and we discussed the design.

The colour scheme of the wedding was burgundy and white, with a theme of hearts, and the dress came out beautifully. It was white, off the shoulder, with burgundy piping round a sweetheart neck and under the bust and was teamed with a little burgundy jacket that covered my shoulders. The skirt was A line and looked really plain so Nina decorated it with a big heart shape in red diamantes with the initials DM for Darren Mansell appliquéd inside it in small rhinestones. All the tables in the marquee were named after hotels in Las Vegas where we were going for our honeymoon and we had casino chips taped inside the name plates which people could take to the bar to exchange for a drink. There were also half-bottles of wine on the tables with our picture and date of wedding on them, non-alcoholic drinks for the children and champagne for the toasts.

I waited until July for replies to my invitations from my family but most of them, including my parents, didn't reply and I had to text them to find out for sure. I was stabbed in the heart when my brother and my aunts, who had always been my champions and friends, said they couldn't come. Reluctantly, I cancelled the order at the tailor's for my brother's suit and asked Duncan to escort me down the aisle.

I was really anxious about what I would do if my dad did turn up after all. I felt I couldn't say to Duncan at the last minute that my father would take over, but I knew Duncan would feel that he had to step down. But Darren said that if my father came, he would have to be a spectator and could come in the barn if there was room, but he would not be giving me away. And I realised he was right: if my father couldn't be bothered even to reply, I shouldn't worry about it.

I asked Chrisman to be toastmaster and Sandra, also from Woodcraft, to do the reading, "The Colour of Love". She is a really special person who has a way of saying things, very calm, angel-like is the only way I can describe it. Jill, a Woodcraft friend, was very touched to be asked to do the other reading: "The Art of Good Marriage". Then we re-did the table plans, replacing all the family with friends, but left four spare places as I still hoped some of them would change their minds and come to wish me well on my special day.

The day before the wedding I told Darren he couldn't stay that night at my house, it was not done. He couldn't see the logic in it as we'd been living together for ages but I kicked him out anyway and he went off to the local Holiday Inn where friends from Scotland, Wales and Yorkshire were gathering. Emma was home from America after a couple of days of drama involving the airline losing her luggage and her having to go up to Preston, where she is at university, to retake an exam, and she had brought several friends who were slumped around the lounge.

On the day of the wedding the hairdresser arrived at 9 a.m. but Emma's hair straighteners were in her lost luggage so she had to shoot off to another salon. The hairdresser put my hair up and it looked beautiful and we were all ready to set off for the barn at 11 a.m. The marquee looked wonderful. I had arranged for helium balloons in burgundy and ivory to be floating along the ridge of the tent and for three balloons to be tied to each table, which was simple but very effective.

At the registration table in the barn we had an archway covered in flowers – artificial ones because Darren suffers from extreme hay fever. He had wanted to carry me over the threshold after the ceremony but I thought, not a good idea, too dangerous. It could have resulted in disaster with the two of us sprawled on the floor in front of all our guests. But thinking about it, it would have made me laugh, oh what a sight. So the archway was a symbolic threshold which we walked through on our way in as single people, then came back through together afterwards as a married couple.

I used a wheelchair which rises up so I was at the same height as Darren and the dress looked fantastic. My bridesmaids, dressed in burgundy, were Emma, Darren's daughters Natalie and Stacey, and one of my carers, Maria. Darren didn't look at me when I came down the aisle as he had been told by his best man it was unlucky but as I reached his side, he turned, looked into my face and broke into a huge, delighted grin.

We had cut out the words "honour and obey" from the marriage ceremony, which was conducted by the registrar. Instead we promised to "respect each other as individuals". Jill and Sandra both did an excellent job with the readings, very moving, then the registrar pronounced us Mr and Mrs Mansell and everyone clapped.

It was a gorgeous day for the photographs on the bridge but it was only just wide enough for my wheelchair. I had to twist it so I didn't fall off but even so there was only an inch in it and I thought that at any moment someone is going to fall against me and push me over the edge and I would be floundering in the lake in my lovely white dress. But luckily, and thanks to the great care taken by the staff at the barn, it didn't happen.

Everyone was called in to the reception and when they were seated, we came in and the atmosphere was wonderful. We had the buffet of cold turkey, beef, ham, salmon, quiches and salads and delicious puddings, then came the speeches.

Chrisman was really funny – he said he had been asked to be the toastmaster, then he brought out a toaster and he said he had been practising for ages but no one seemed to want any toast. Duncan was shaking when he gave his speech in which he said, "I am not Louise's dad. Unfortunately, her dad isn't here." It brought tears to my eyes as I looked at the four empty spaces we had saved in hope and thought, he should have been here. Darren spoke and I gave a short speech too in which I said that this morning I had two children, a boy and a girl, and now I have four: I have three girls and a boy.

Apart from my family not coming, it was the wedding day of my dreams. Grahame Tindale, my childhood friend from Chailey, who was the equivalent of family to me, was there and I was so pleased to see him and we had lots of people from Woodcraft and Darren's football connections.

We had a disco and a band, led by the owner of the barn who used to play in a Sixties band called Strange Brew, who were really good. The atmosphere was so warm and joyful – there was no strain, no tension, no animosity, no bad feeling, everybody was dancing and getting on with everybody else.

Darren and I started the dancing with a slow number: Elton John's "Can You Feel the Love Tonight?" As we took to the floor, the best man popped a big balloon which was suspended over our heads and inside it were lots of little balloons and loads of confetti which cascaded down on us as we cuddled and swayed together.

As it got near midnight, Darren said we should all sing "Bog Down in the Valley-o," a popular Woodcraft Folk song, it had been sung at his Stag night in Dublin, so we did that, and then I thought it would be really nice to finish in the traditional Woodcraft way with the theme song "Link Your Hands Together". So I bellowed, "Woodcraft!" as only I can, and we all got in a big circle and took each others' hands and sang this lovely song. Then we had a conga which I was at the head of but I had had a bit too much to drink so it didn't go as well as it should have, and we fell into bed at about 2 a.m. There are no words to describe how happy I was.

The next day we had breakfast with everyone, then left for home. I had suspected that my friends would do something daft with our car but I thought I had thwarted them by leaving the keys in my room and keeping my room key on me all the time. But I forgot that I'd left a window open. One of our friends had climbed in, got my car keys and let off a couple of confetti bombs inside, wound white ribbon all round the steering wheel and gear stick and tied a couple of cans on the back which made an appalling racket all the way home. It was a terrible mess but very nice.

That day we sorted out presents and the following

morning at 5 a.m. we left for our honeymoon in Las Vegas. It was a seven-hour flight to New York, a five-hour wait at the airport and another five-hour flight to Vegas. Since I can't get to the loo on an aeroplane but have to drink enough to keep my transplanted kidney functioning, it was all a bit tricky, but I managed.

As soon as we arrived in Vegas, we took our stuff to our junior penthouse on the 30th floor in the MGM Grand Signature hotel, and hit the town. Over the next two weeks we saw fabulous shows like Mamma Mia! and Cher, played the slot machines, toured the hotels which all had different exotic attractions like white lions in an enclosure in the grounds, golden alligators, white tigers, flamingos or dancing fountains, and usually ate just the starter of the enormous American meals.

We also went to the Titanic exhibition which was very emotional. Everyone got a boarding card as they went in with the name of a real person and the class they travelled in. You went round displays of how the ship was built and reproductions of different areas of it and at the end there was a big wall with all the passengers' names on, where you looked for the fate of your character. Mine was a woman from Cornwall who was travelling with her children to start a new life in the US. She was in second class and she survived while Darren's was a man from Norway in third class who didn't make it.

It was a perfect honeymoon: for the whole two weeks we got on so well and we managed by ourselves without a carer. We thought we might have trouble with my hair getting tangled but Darren washed it by pouring shampoo on which he spread around with a body brush. Then he put lots of conditioner on and brushed it through to get out all the knots. The only problem we did have was a build up of static from the nylon carpets they have everywhere – we kept giving each other electric shocks and my hair stood on end like Worzel Gummidge.

There was one disappointment in that I was desperate to go to the Grand Canyon but no one would take me in my electric wheelchair. Darren searched up and down the town and investigated every possible way to get me there. I thought to myself, he is so caring and this is one reason why I married him. He asked all the tour operators he could find but they said it was a scooter and they couldn't carry it. We could have flown over, but not landed, or landed in a helicopter but there would have been no chair at the other end. Eventually we heard of somewhere we could hire a van but they needed three days notice and we only had two left. I was devastated and very shocked. Americans have got such good disability rights usually, yet they got away with this. I was really upset, angry and frustrated and when I got home I wrote a letter of protest to the US embassy.

Reflections

This book is not about me airing grievances. I don't want anyone to feel I am getting at them, I don't want to hurt anyone. But the thalidomide story is unique in history – at least, one hopes so – and I feel it needs to be recorded how I and other Thalidomiders were treated and brought up and how we have overcome the circumstances of our birth.

While I haven't nursed a grievance through my life against the Distillers Company, or Chemie Grumenthal which first invented thalidomide, the new research into the real truth of the development of thalidomide may cause me to feel quite differently about them.

In any case, I am only human and I confess sometimes to having felt bitter that, through the negligent and greedy actions of a handful of men, I lost out on being with my family when I was a child. And I felt bitter when my own children were small that I had not the arms to pick them up and cuddle them when they were crying. But as I look back over my life, I feel I have achieved what any other average person, disabled or able-bodied, generally achieves. I'm no different, I'm just getting on with my life, and I don't want to lead it clouded by bitterness.

On my birth and the way I ended up in Chailey, I can see in hindsight that it was not my parents' fault that they didn't bond with me. It was the hospital regime of the time to assume a newly delivered mother was exhausted and to take the baby away, and to put disabled babies in homes. Now they realise how important it is for mother and child to be brought together straight away, probably even more so if there is a problem. Technology and the understanding of the human body and mind have come a long way since the 60s.

I have never blamed my mother for taking thalidomide; it was just one of those things. In fact, I feel sorry for my mum in the sense that the society of the time didn't do her justice. She needed people around her to be strong, to support her as she faced, at 21, being a mother to a thalidomide baby, and society didn't do that. Doctors and social workers were the worst culprits of all and I feel bitter that my mum was deprived of the support that she would be given if it happened now.

For most of my life I have felt humble and honoured to be my dad's daughter because of all that he has done for me and the other Thalidomiders. My family has benefited very much from his generosity; the kids have been on five-star holidays and luxury cruises, he has given them lavish presents and helped pay the school fees for two years, for which I am very grateful.

I feel that all the difficult stages we have gone through in our relationship have been caused by the fact that my birth was an injury to his sense of masculine pride, that he has a very Victorian, patriarchal, controlling personality and by the fact that we are so similar! He led the way in the fight for compensation and has given hope to people round the world that they might yet get something, and it was all done by this very stubborn, independent, hurt, man. So I am proud to be his daughter.

On all the mauling about I was subjected to as I was growing up which I hated so much: the examinations and tests and photographs and medicals and the way we were expected to wear artificial legs and arms, I do realise they did it from an attitude of care. Chailey Heritage was renowned for the contraptions they invented and for their determination to make their charges independent. They were extremely good at it, but growing up in any institution or boarding school is hard whether you are able-bodied or disabled.

At the time I went to Chailey, attitudes to disabled people were changing, from those prevalent since Victorian times that they should be provided with a comfortable life in institutions separate and hidden from the rest of society, to the modern idea that they should be members of the normal community. Chailey was going through a steep learning curve when I was there and finding it really difficult to reconcile its beliefs and what it was founded for with the new ideas of the way it should operate in the present day.

You can teach children what order to use their cutlery in at the dinner table, but you can't teach the unwritten rules of family life because they cannot be defined and written down, so that was where we lost out. On the positive side, it welded us together as a community and very successfully taught us to be independent and to speak our minds. Now Chailey has changed in many ways, particularly that they are more child-friendly and house people in small, family units.

Looking back on the time I left Chailey and started life on my own; I still cannot understand why my parents thought, because I would not do what they wanted me to, that they were not going to talk to me and I was not allowed to go home. I find it really shocking and heartbreaking even now when I think about the two days I was homeless in London and the lonely holidays I spent in that horrible YWCA.

Yet you learn from everything, and it did teach me to respect people on the streets. I can say I have been there, even for a short time. I know how it feels to be unwanted, not to have a place in the world, not to be able to say, ooh, I think I'll sit down with a cup of tea and put my feet up. The only place you have is where you are standing at that moment.

Despite the way my marriage to John ended, meeting him was a godsend; I loved him very, very dearly and for many years we got on so well. In hindsight, maybe I should have listened to my instincts on the morning of my wedding day which were telling me, "Don't get out of bed!" and not gone ahead. But I don't regret it because I've got two wonderful children and I had good times as well as bad: after all, that's what you have got to expect in marriage.

I am extremely proud of Emma and Jack, the way they manage having me as a mother. I know that in their eyes I am Mum; it doesn't matter if you are spherical with pink spots, your kids love you for what you are. But I am aware that some people have picked on my kids because I am disabled and, now that I am with Darren, they have got two disabled parents and one step-dad. That can be awkward for them and I am proud of the way they cope.

I am proud that I have achieved a lot with young people through my talks in schools and being a leader of the Woodcraft Folk. The kids who have been members in Cheltenham in the 14 years I have been active have known me for what I am and consequently their attitudes to disabled people are more open. I feel that I have made youngsters realise that they must treat disabled people the way they would like to be treated themselves if one day they got run over by a bus and found themselves in a wheelchair. And that I have shown them that it would not change who they are, just what they are capable of doing.

My relationships with animals have had a very special place in my life and I still feel I have a particular bond with them. Much of the time I would rather be with animals than humans, as they give you unconditional love and you can give them unconditional love in return.

I especially love German shepherds. I usually have two but I've only got one at the moment, Ajay, who is four years old and a real handful as he is over-protective of me. You have to respect German shepherds because they could kill you if they chose but they give you endless affection, are great company and always there for you. I have such fond memories of dogs I have had which have now passed on that I keep all their ashes in a cupboard in my bedroom and have instructed my family that, after I have died and been cremated, they must pour them into the pot with mine and bury us all together.

Ever since I moved into my own home, I have had carers and I want to say a big thank you to all of them. If it hadn't been for their assistance and their enthusiasm and their charm and their sense of humour – you need a sense of humour to be anywhere near me – and their tolerance, I would not be where I am today. I would not be living an independent life, bringing up my kids in a normal environment.

I started with Community Service Volunteers then moved on to nannies, mother's helps, and now personal assistants from Slovakia. I've had lots and lots of carers, good and bad, including a drug addict, an alcoholic, one who had been here two months when she discovered she was pregnant and people who have tried to take advantage of me. But from 1981 I've only ever sacked two, and that's not bad at all.

Getting along in this situation is an art and it has got to be both ways. What I make clear to them is that the way they help me look after my kids, is that they look after me, and I look after the kids. They have got to be caring, first and foremost, and they have a lot to contend with: my attitude and the way I was brought up comes through and I can be very stubborn and not particularly nice. They have to accept that this is MY home so they can't try to rule the roost; I am boss. I am a fair boss, I like messing around and having fun but they work for me, they have got to get on with me, the kids, Darren, the dogs and with each other, as I have two at once.

Some of the things they have done are hilarious. My first one, Nicky, who became a great friend, was on a gap year and had never cooked in her life. She once asked me how many peas I wanted and, being a bit sarcastic in those days, I said 102. Five minutes later I went in the kitchen and asked her what she was doing and she said, "I've got up to 50" – she was counting them!

Another one swore she knew how to do housework so I left her to the vacuuming but after the machine had been going for 20 minutes in Emma's room, I went to investigate. She switched it off with a look of relief so I asked what was wrong and she said, "Oh, my arms are killing me!" She had lifted the vacuum off the ground and was swishing it around two inches above the floor.

After I had sorted her out there, the kitchen and bathroom

were next and I soon heard a great sloshing noise. I hurried to the kitchen to find the floor was flooded. "Did you have an accident?" I asked. "No, I'm just wiping the floor," she said. She had thrown a whole bucket of water over the floor and was on her hands and knees wiping it up with a towel. I showed her how to do it with the mop but it took an hour to dry by which time the dogs had come skating in from outside, skidded across the floor, knocked into the bin which fell over and spilled out yesterday's dinner so she had to do it all over again. I went back to the computer then all of a sudden I heard another whoosh – she'd only gone and thrown another bucket of water over the bathroom floor. I gave up.

Reflecting on my second marriage, I confess that the fact my parents stuck to their resolve not to come to my wedding has changed my attitude to them. I feel that all my life I have been protecting my family, making excuses for them. I have mulled over why they did not bring me up themselves, said to myself it was because of society's attitudes, it was not their fault, they were too young. But when a time came that was very important to me, that was supposed to be a joyful occasion bringing families together, my father showed his true colours.

It was instilled in me by my father that you should respect your parents, as I do, but surely somewhere along the line your parents have to respect you as an individual. I am not a child any more, and because they snubbed my wedding, the respect and loyalty I had for them has been damaged.

In future they will have to get in touch with me if they want contact. If they do, they will find the door is not completely closed against them. I know people don't change, they are as they are, but there should always be hope. Darren says I am too soft but I say that if they want to push the door, they will find that it will swing open. It's just that they might have to push it a bit harder than they've been used to up to now.

I have found my soul-mate in Darren. I should have listened to my heart when we were first together all those years ago but I am just thankful that we came together again. Yes, we have our differences and I am not the easiest person to live with. I can be very argumentative and hard to get on with but I think he will manage me. I hope so, anyway.

In the future I will continue being a Woodcraft leader, giving lectures and doing my campaigning work on behalf of thalidomide victims round the world and Darren and I want to travel. Next year we plan to celebrate our first anniversary by flying to New York then going on an Amtrak train to Washington.

Most importantly, though, Darren and I want to grow old together and to be there for our children. Our family is reaching a new stage as the children become adults and, because I have always found creating a normal family life difficult, I feel I have got more learning to do.

Through watching other families I have worked out the way I think parents should behave towards their adult children; I don't want to be a control freak, I just want to be there for them and to support them in whatever they want to do. It is my next ambition – let's see if I can achieve it!

I have to say that, though life has occasionally been hard to bear, most of the time it doesn't really matter that I have "no hand to hold and no legs to dance on", as I have made do with what I have. I have life, laughter, friendship, companionship from all the animals that have helped me over the years and especially LOVE from Emma, Jack and now Darren.

I started writing this book some twenty-one years ago. I have stopped from time to time mainly because it became too painful to write as it reminded me that I hadn't had an ordinary experience in life or family. I told my family that I was writing it, not to show off, nor to get back at the way things went in my life, but mainly to tell you that The Thalidomide Experience wasn't just about the hero stuff in the way that we have all overcome obstacles that nobody thought we would. It was also to give an insight into how we Thalidomiders experienced society's Victorian ideas of how disabled people – also called "the handicapped" or just plain "freaks" – should be hidden away. We owe huge thanks to people like Lord Jack Ashley, Sir David English, Sir Harold Evans and the Insight team at *The Sunday Times*, who brought the thalidomide story to the public. Also to my dad because, if it hadn't been for him, none of us would have had the life we are still living.

A special thanks to Gill Swain, who from about the year 2000 has sat through hours of me talking, sometimes crying, as she wrote my words. She has, I hope, managed to bring my story to life as well as conveying a taste of life for disabled people being brought up in institutions in the 1960s.

As I enter my new life with my soulmate and husband, Darren, I look forward to holding his hands, which are no longer than mine, as we walk towards the future together and dancing with him in my wheelchair that rises. Never more will it be "no hand to hold and no legs to dance on".